RECREATION

THROUGH

MUSIC

PREFACE

Recreation represents a universal need of human beings. Throughout history, people have sought worth-while and satisfying forms of recreation as an emotional outlet, for personal fulfillment, and for the attainment of pleasure. The development of the modern social and economic structure has produced increased leisure time, an accelerated tempo of living, and a multitude of destructive tensions and frustrations, all of which constitute serious problems for society. All levels of society—the individual, the family, and private, public, and governmental agencies—have joined forces to meet these problems. As a result, the recreation movement, during the past few years, has had unprecedented growth.

Responsiveness to music is a basic human characteristic. Music has universal appeal and has been traditionally one of the principal forms of recreation. In order to utilize to the fullest the unique contributions and the infinite potentialities of music as recreation, the recreation movement requires leaders who like music, understand something about it, and appreciate what it can do for people.

This book seeks to provide a basic orientation in the recreational music program. It is addressed to three groups of people, all musical laymen—individuals who wish to participate more actively in recreational music, students and teachers of recreation courses, and professional recreation leaders.

I wish to express my appreciation to Professor John L. Hutchinson, Teachers College, Columbia University, for his valuable assistance in the general field of recreation; and to Professor Howard A. Murphy, also of Teachers College, for his constructive criticism of the material on listening. Special acknowledgment is due C. G. Conn, Ltd., Elkhart, Indiana; Linton Manufacturing Company, Inc., Elkhart, Indiana; Carl Fischer Musical Instrument Co., Inc., New York; Fred Gretsch Manufacturing Co., Brooklyn; Pan-

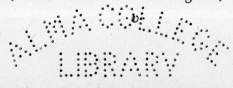

Preface

American Band Instrument Co., Elkhart, Indiana; and Oscar Schmidt-International, Newark, New Jersey, for providing the many excellent photographs of instruments. Finally, I am most grateful to my wife, Patricia, for her constant encouragement and for her penetrating evaluation of the text from the point of view of the musical amateur.

CHARLES LEONHARD

Urbana, Illinois
January, 1952

CONTENTS

Contents

DIAGRAMS

PHOTOGRAPHS

Illustrations will be found between pages 20 and 21.

Photographs

RECREATION

THROUGH

MUSIC

CHAPTER ONE

RECREATION AND

MUSIC

Throughout history, people of all cultures have longed and strived for a reduction in the number of their working hours. Technological advances affecting business, industry, and agriculture, along with social pressure, have made the forty-hour week a reality in the United States. Furthermore, present trends indicate that the work week will be shortened even more in the years ahead. In order to be a well-adjusted, contented, and productive member of society, a person must employ his leisure time in a worthy and constructive manner.

The results of an individual's work are definite and tangible: through it he attains the material things necessary to sustain life. Many people find considerable personal satisfaction in their vocations too, but for others the process of gaining a livelihood is full of frustration and dissatisfaction. The technological developments that have shortened the work week have resulted in a significant increase in the number of people who find little or no personal satisfaction or opportunity for self-expression in their work. If a person does not gain satisfaction and self-realization in his work, it is essential that he secure them outside his work. Likewise, the vocationally satisfied individual needs enriching leisure time experiences to assure a well-rounded life.

The ever-increasing amount of leisure time, therefore, creates an emergent social problem. An aimless, unsocial use of leisure can have only a destructive effect upon the individual and his community. A thoughtful, constructive use of leisure can make a vital contribution to the personal development of the individual and to the cultural advancement of society.

At one time the home and the family were the major forces in the use of leisure time. With the decrease in the size of families and the increase in urban living, the potentialities for recreation in the home have been somewhat reduced, but the home remains a focal point in the use of leisure time. Churches, clubs, lodges, and other organizations have always played an important part in the use of leisure time and continue to do so. In recent years, recreation as a public service has been recognized as a function of government. Organizations for the direction of recreation activities have been formed at the local, county, state, and federal levels.

It is clear that a constructive use of leisure time has important and far-reaching social implications and that the problem must be considered intelligently on all levels of society, by the individual, by the family, by educational, religious, and social organizations, and by governmental agencies.

RECREATION DEFINED

Recreation is a voluntary leisure experience which is acceptable to society and which provides immediate and long-range satisfactions for the person who participates in it. Recreation is possible only in a permissive atmosphere. To be recreative, an experience must be voluntary and the individual who participates in the experience must do so because he desires to participate. Rigid rules of conduct, restrictions, and unnecessary controls are not conducive to recreation.

The form of recreation must be acceptable to society and consistent with the mores of the people. A good recreation program evolves from the interests, ideals, attitudes, and customs of the people involved, and is based on their needs. The most desirable forms of recreation give the individual both immediate and long-range satisfaction. The first requisite of recreation is that it satisfy the participant immediately. Unless an experience is pleasant from the beginning, there is little likelihood that he will continue it. On the other hand, an activity, no matter how pleasant initially, that fails to offer the participant a challenge beyond his initial accomplishment will not hold his interest for long. If he can see possibilities for developing skill and knowledge, he attains satisfaction throughout the participation process, from an elementary level through the various stages toward skilled performance and mastery of techniques.

THE OBJECTIVES OF
RECREATION

The objectives of recreation are enjoyment by all the participants, the development and fulfillment of the potentialities of the individual, and the enrichment of the social group.

The attainment of pleasure and enjoyment is implicit in recreation and is the primary objective of any recreation experience. An experience that is painful or upsetting, physically or emotionally, can by no means be considered recreational; it is, rather, destructive and harmful. Many people destroy the recreational value of an activity by becoming overly serious and developing a perfectionist attitude toward their performance. People who engage in overstrenuous athletics or who develop temper tantrums over a game of cards are examples which are far too common.

Recreation serves as a means of developing an individual's potentialities and provides an opportunity for self-expression. Everyone has numerous latent or undeveloped capacities and talents which he does not use in the course of common day-to-day living. Early in life a person makes a vocational choice. He thereafter may bend every effort toward perfecting the skills and attaining the knowledge necessary for success. It often happens that many of his talents, interests, and means of expression are subordinated to his vocational development, with the result that he is less than the complete human being he might be. Through a wise choice of recreation experiences in his leisure time the individual can capitalize on his aptitudes and interests and thus can realize more fully his innate potentialities.

In a democratic society, every individual has definite responsibilities toward the social group and can make a contribution to the enrichment of society. An organized recreation program provides an excellent opportunity for human interaction and for promoting unity and understanding among the many different groups which make up society. The recreation program can serve as a laboratory for democratic action in that individual skills, capacities, and talents are shared in attaining common goals.

MUSIC AS RECREATION

Music may be approached from several points of view. For some people it is a profession and a life work; for some it serves as a part of a religious service; for others it is a business or commercial enterprise; but for most it is a form of recreation.

Music is almost without a peer as a medium for recreation. Its appeal is so wide and its possibilities so infinite that its recreational potentialities can never be exhausted.

Music is eminently acceptable to society. Every known culture in the history of the world has developed some characteristic and original form of musical expression. In Western civilization music has undergone the greatest development in history and is an integral part of the cultural heritage. The United States is a musical country and in recent years has become in many respects the music center of the world.

Experience in music brings both immediate and long-range satisfaction. Nearly everyone is musical to a degree and can find immediate pleasure and satisfaction in some form of musical participation. On the other hand, music is a subject so profound and so complex that no one ever learns all there is to know about it or ever attains absolute perfection in it. In music there is for everyone a continuing challenge, new fields to explore, and new techniques to master. The more a person knows about music, the more he wants to learn, and the more pleasure he gains from it.

Music has appeal for people of all ages. Children make musical sounds before they can talk. Their first attempts at vocal expression result in the production of tone and the sounding of intervals of pitch used in music. They begin to respond to tone at the age of three months and are soothed and pleased by music. This basic responsiveness, which remains with them all through life, is the foundation for all kinds of musical growth. From infancy to old age, music can play an important part in the life of everyone. Many recreational pursuits are closed to elderly people because they require too much physical exertion, but many musical experiences are possible regardless of age or infirmity. No kind of musical participation requires violent physical exertion.

Participation in music can begin at any age. Musical talent may lie dormant for years, then undergo startling development when the possessor encounters a favorable musical environment. Although playing instruments and singing require the development of intricate motor skills and are best started at an early age, many adults start and make fine progress in both activities and derive great satisfaction from them. Maturity lends depth and meaning to all musical experiences, particularly to listening. Experience in living heightens emotional responsiveness to music. A person can continue to experience and enjoy music until the end of his life.

The outstanding characteristic of music is its expressiveness. All the emotions, moods, aspirations, hopes, and fears of the human race have been expressed in music. The vehicles for expression range all the way from the simplest of folk songs to the most exalted symphonic and choral compositions. Music has the power to take a person out of himself, out of the humdrum of day-to-day existence, and to arouse in his heart the most joyous and noblest emotions. Through music he can recreate for himself, and make part of his experience, the excitement, the despair, the joy, or whatever emotion impelled the composer to write the music or the folk to improvise it. Through music a person can attain the quintessence of beauty, walk the Olympian heights of nobility and exultation, or drain the bitterest dregs of remorse and anguish. The essence of music is life itself. To experience the finest of music is to experience life in a measure and fashion beyond the limits of the usual spiritual and emotional resources. Such experience brings a person into contact with one of the most significant aspects of Western culture, broadens his point of view, and may assist him in attaining the emotional stability so essential for happiness. Music is one of the most beautiful things in life. It is every man's right to experience it to the full extent of his ability.

Music is ever present and always available. Everyone has musical resources within himself. He can sing or play an instrument and attain satisfaction and pleasure, or he can listen to the music of his choice in his own home. When his resources are combined with those of other people in an organized or informal group, the possibilities are greatly increased. The group may be small or large: it may consist of a family or a circle of friends, or it may be drawn from the entire community. Modern means of communication have literally brought the world of music into every home. The radio, the phonograph, and television have all contributed to the development of a music-conscious and musically literate public. The public schools and other educational institutions are also doing a great deal to cultivate the musical interest and ability of the student and community population.

The responsibility for directing the musical experience of all segments of the population lies with the professional recreation leader. There is a great need for musicians who understand and are interested in recreation and for workers in recreation who have an interest in and know something about music. Many musicians find it difficult to adopt a recreational viewpoint about music, and many recreation leaders have little conception of the vital role music can and should play in their recreation programs. A clear understanding of the role of the leader in the music phase of the recreation program will assist both groups in contributing to the effectiveness of recreation through music.

THE RECREATION LEADER
AND MUSIC

The recreation leader should be aware of the recreational possibilities of music. He should cultivate his own interest in music and develop his innate musical capacities. He should discover and utilize all the human resources available to him, including professional musicians and music educators who are interested in recreation and qualified to work in that area, and interested, talented lay persons who are enthusiastic about music and want to help others gain experience in it. He should discover people with latent musical talent and encourage and help them to develop it. Only in this way can he organize and develop a recreational music program that will enrich to the fullest the lives of all those whom he serves. In directing the music program, the recreation leader should concern himself with three phases of music—listening, singing, and playing.

It is essential that the different music activities in the recreation program be well integrated. The instrumental and vocal ensembles can contribute to the listening program, and the individual instrumentalists or groups can serve as accompanists for community singing and for choral organizations. The music program must be adapted to the situation and must grow out of the needs of the people for whom it is planned.

The Listening Program

In developing the listening program, the recreation leader must explore for himself the pleasure of listening to music and learn as much about it as possible. He should secure the best possible equipment and facilities—phonographs, radios, television sets, recordings, and rooms adequate for their use. It is his responsibility to arrange and publicize concerts and recitals, plan regularly scheduled programs of recorded music, organize music appreciation classes conducted by qualified persons, and make available facilities for informal listening by individuals and small groups. He provides information concerning music programs in the community and on the radio and television. He sets up a library of recordings for loan or rental. He establishes liaison with professional musicians as well as with the music personnel in the schools, churches, clubs, and other organizations in the community. He plans a listening program sufficiently broad and varied to meet the needs of all ages and of all levels of musical taste.

The Singing Program

In developing the singing program, the recreation leader should participate actively by singing and leading singing. He should encourage community singing in both small and large groups, and foster the development of choral music and the organization of choral groups of all kinds—mixed choruses, men's glee clubs, women's glee clubs, quartets, trios, and other small singing groups. He secures the services of specialists to direct the choral groups. He arranges regular and adequate rehearsal time and opportunities for public performances by the choral groups. He sees that the program provides for the development of special ability, through the organization of voice classes. He sponsors the production of operettas and light operas. He sets up a library of music which includes choral music, songbooks, song slides, and song sheets for community singing.

The Playing Program

Due to the technical nature of playing instruments, the role of the recreation leader in the playing program is principally one of organization and administration, unless he is a music specialist. The playing program consists of various instrumental ensembles, orchestras, bands, chamber music groups, and class instruction in instruments. In recent years the development of effective techniques has made class instruction in instrumental music desirable and quite economical. Such instruction contributes greatly to the development of the instrumental ensembles. There is always tremendous interest in the piano class among both adults and children, making it a proper part of every recreation program. It is also desirable to offer instruction in the simpler instruments, such as the guitar, banjo, ukelele and auto-harp. These instruments are easy to play and, in addition to creating an immediate feeling of accomplishment and satisfaction, are an excellent point of departure for learning to read music and to play the more complex instruments. .

Succeeding chapters treat each phase of the recreational music program in detail.

CHAPTER TWO

RECREATION

THROUGH

LISTENING

Composers and performers, by joint effort, are the producers of music. Listeners are the consumers of music and are necessary for the fulfillment of both composers and performers.

Listening to music is the kind of musical participation in which everyone can engage and is a most satisfying form of recreation. A person can listen to music alone or among a large audience, in a concert hall or in his own living room. He can listen in the presence of the performer, to the radio or television, or through the medium of recordings. Under any of these circumstances his reaction to music is subjective and the experience can be recreative in the best meaning of the word.

If listening to music is to have optimum value as recreation, a person must know something about how to listen. The recreational value of listening to music is dubious if the listener is inattentive or if he hears the music only as a background for conversation or other activities. If he wants to attain the utmost in pleasure and enjoyment, the listener needs to know something about the nature of music and the elements that make music what it is. He needs to know what to listen for and where to focus his attention. He must be acquainted with the various styles in music, the different types of compositions, and the composers who have contributed to the vast storehouse of music literature. In other words, he needs to develop a degree of musical awareness and musical literacy. The purpose of this chapter is to present some general information which will help the layman gain such an understanding of music.

ELEMENTS OF MUSIC

Music is organized sound. The nature of the organization and the quality of the sound differentiate music from noise. The sound from which music is made is tone. Tone may be defined as sound dominated by a pitch component. In music, there is a ceaseless alternation between movement of tone and rest. The movement of tone creates intensity in varying degrees, and complete relaxation from the intensity comes with rest. The emotional and expressive content of music is projected through the creation of intensity followed by relaxation. Responsiveness to music depends upon a sensitivity to the constant undulations between intensity and relaxation and to the rhythm, melody, harmony, form, and tone color of the music.

Rhythm, melody, harmony, form, and tone color are the components of music, the materials from which the composer makes music. They are all so closely interrelated that it is virtually impossible to isolate any one from the others. They all affect one another and never act separately. Nevertheless, for purposes of analysis and explanation, each is treated here in turn.

Rhythm

Mursell has defined rhythm as "a pattern of stress, release, duration, and pause organized for an expressive purpose." [1] The significance of this definition lies in its emphasis on the expressive quality of rhythm. The hammering of an expert carpenter has sufficient regularity to be rhythmic but the fact that its purpose is to drive a nail rather than to express feeling or emotion differentiates it from rhythm. Rhythm is expressive and has universal appeal. The beating of a tom-tom for dancing by an aboriginal tribe is rhythmic and undeniably expressive. The power of rhythm is irresistible.

---

[1] James L. Mursell, *Education for Musical Growth* (Boston: Ginn and Company, 1948), p. 44.

All music has rhythm. The function of rhythm is to measure in space-time the forward motion of the music. In dance music rhythm is more prominent than in other types of music. In Ravel's *Bolero,* for example, there is a constant, insistent repetition of a rhythmic pattern which dominates the entire composition and results in tremendous excitement and intensity.

In listening to music a person should be aware of the rhythm and should respond to it both physically and emotionally. A good starting point for learning to listen to music is to hear compositions that are highly rhythmic. The waltzes of Johann Strauss and the waltzes, mazurkas, and polonaises of Chopin are all dance forms in which the rhythm is clear-cut and exciting.

Melody

Melody, the horizonal element of musical texture, may be defined as a succession of musical tones. Such a definition, however, is inadequate. A melody is a dynamic, living thing. Every melody flows through many different tones, but the tones do not make the melody; they are only the points through which the melody passes. A person's response to melody is not a response to the separate notes; it is a response to the melody as a whole.[2]

Melodies move in units called *phrases.* In each phrase the tones rise and fall and at the end of each phrase there is a pause in the flow of the melody. The musical term for this pause is *cadence.* Most phrases consist of two or more small fragments called *motives* or *figures.* Perhaps the most familiar motive in music literature is the first four notes of Beethoven's *Fifth Symphony,* often called "Fate knocking at the door."

The first phrase of *America* is made up of three figures or motives. The first figure is on the words "My country, 'tis of thee." On the words "Sweet land of liberty," the second figure begins with the same rhythm and melody on a higher pitch, but the last three notes move downward instead of upward as in the first figure. On the words "Of thee I sing," a new and different figure

[2] Mursell, *ibid.,* p. 41.

moves gently down to the cadence. This phrase provides a simple demonstration of the characteristics of all good melodies: balance, unity, and variety.

Melody is the means by which much of the movement and intensity of music is attained. As the tones of a melody rise, there is a feeling of intensity; as they fall, there is a feeling of repose. The melody contains much of the emotional message of music; melody is the element which is most striking and most easily grasped. Some melodies are easy to comprehend and stay in one's mind and ear after a very few hearings. Other melodies require numerous hearings before they can be learned and remembered, but repeated and acute listening makes these more complex melodies as clear and understandable as the simplest folk tune. The inexperienced listener should begin his musical experience with music that contains attractive, singable melodies. Compositions based on folk music are ideal in this respect.

Harmony

Harmony, the vertical element of musical texture, is closely related to melody and is inseparable from it. Harmony consists of chords, or combinations of tones, which support the melody. Every melody has its own harmonic implications—that is, each melody suggests to the musical ear chords which color and enrich its expressive value. Many people hear harmony when they sing or whistle a melody.

Harmony itself has expressive value. Some chords are sweetly consonant and give an effect of repose while others are harshly dissonant and build up a feeling of intensity which seeks rest and completion.

Consonance and dissonance are the foundation of harmonic music. The words are difficult to define. Consonance is used to describe the agreeable effect of repose produced by certain chords; dissonance, the disagreeable effect of disturbance produced by other chords. Consonance and dissonance are not absolute qualities. A chord has the effect of dissonance only when heard in relation to chords surrounding it that are less dissonant. A certain chord gives the effect of dissonance when placed among some chords and the effect of consonance when placed among other chords. The purest consonance in harmony is the so-called "chord of nature," the major chord: C-E-G-C.

One of the most significant developments in the history of music has been the increasing use of dissonant harmony. In church music of the early part of the Christian era no dissonances were permitted. The music of the seventeenth and eighteenth centuries contains dissonant harmonies, but the dissonant chords are carefully and scrupulously resolved to consonant chords. During the nineteenth century new dissonant chords were added to harmonic usage and there was much greater freedom in the use of dissonance. Contemporary music abounds in dissonance. Many chords which would have been considered shockingly dissonant in the eighteenth or even the nineteenth century have an effect of consonance in contemporary music when heard in relation to the surrounding harmony.

Form

All the arts have form. In the visual arts, the plastic arts, and architecture, the form is concrete; it can be seen, understood, and appreciated at a glance. Form in music is more abstract. When listening to music, one must grasp the form immediately as its elements unfold.

Daniel Gregory Mason, the eminent American composer and scholar, once said, "Form is to music what plot is to a story; it is the order in which things happen." [3] Form in music is the organization of parts in a meaningful whole. It is the plan or the framework within which the composer communicates his ideas. The principles governing form in music are repetition, contrast, and balance. Composers write music with form to make it more meaningful, expressive, and enjoyable. When listening to music, a per-

---

[3] Howard A. Murphy, *Form in Music for the Listener* (Camden, N.J.: RCA Victor, 1948), p. ix.

son may increase his pleasure and understanding by noticing repetitions and contrast as the composition unfolds.

The Star Spangled Banner represents one of the forms which reoccur in music and exemplifies the principles common to all musical forms. The words of the first portion follow:

> Oh, say, can you see,
> By the dawn's early light,
> What so proudly we hailed
> At the twilight's last gleaming?

Verbally and musically this portion has meaning. It expresses a complete thought.

On the next four lines of the poem, the music for the first four lines is repeated:

> Whose broad stripes and bright stars,
> Through the perilous fight,
> O'er the ramparts we watched
> Were so gallantly streaming.

This exemplifies the principle of repetition in musical form and makes up the first part of the song.

On the next four lines of poetry the melody is different:

> And the rockets' red glare,
> The bombs bursting in air,
> Gave proof through the night
> That our flag was still there.

This new melodic material exemplifies the principle of contrast and makes up the second part of the song. It leads directly to the last four lines of the stanza for which the melody is still different:

> Oh, say, does that Star Spangled
> Banner yet wave
> O'er the land of the free
> And the home of the brave?

The song is divided into three different parts. The first part announces a melody and repeats it. The second and third parts provide contrast with the first part and with each other. The fact that the first part is the same length as the last two parts taken together gives a feeling of balance.

Old Folks at Home has a different form or design. The melody for the first part is announced on the first two lines of the poem:

> Way down upon the Swannee River,
> Far, far away,

Neither the words nor the music express a complete meaning. They lead directly to the third and fourth lines of the poem:

> There's where my heart is turning ever,
> There's where the old folks stay.

The melody for these words is a repetition of that for the first two lines except that the ending (cadence) is more complete and final. These two phrases taken together have a complete meaning both in a verbal and a musical sense. They make up the first part of the song.

The words for the second part follow:

> All the world is sad and dreary,
> Everywhere I roam.

The music for these words is made up of new material and has a different melody. This second part contrasts with the first part and is called a *departure*. The words express a thought and the music leads to the third part:

> Oh, darkies, how my heart grows weary
> Far from the old folks at home.

The melody for the third part is a repetition of that heard in the first part. Thus, this song is a three-part form.

Letters are often used to designate the different parts in music. A schematic analysis of *Old Folks at Home* follows:

> First part: Statement of the melody—A
> Second part: Departure, new melody—B
> Third part: Return, repetition of first part—A

Many familiar songs, such as *Drink to Me Only with Thine Eyes, Jeannie with the Light Brown Hair, Silver Threads among the Gold,* and *Carry Me Back to Old Virginny,* are written in this same three-part song form. These are simple illustrations, but they are sufficient to demonstrate the principles which govern form in music.[4]

Tone Color

Each musical instrument and each voice has its own characteristic tone color or timbre. Tone color varies with the way in which the tone is produced. Tone is the result of vibrations of a string, a reed, the lips, a column of air, a drum head, or the vocal chords. With careful attention and the development of awareness, anyone can learn to recognize the characteristic tone of all instruments and voices.

The symphony orchestra has almost unlimited tonal resources and reigns supreme as a medium of musical expression. There are more than one hundred instruments in the modern symphony orchestra, divided into four groups: strings, woodwinds or reeds, brasses, and percussion. Diagram 1 shows a common seating arrangement for the symphony orchestra.

STRINGS

The strings are the backbone of the orchestra and constitute about three fifths of the instruments in the modern symphony orchestra. The tone of all the stringed instruments is generally produced by drawing the bow over the strings. The player moves the bow with his right hand and, with his left hand, he presses the strings at different points to obtain various pitches. These instruments operate on the acoustical principle that the pitch produced by a vibrating string depends upon the size and length of the string. The mute, a three-pronged clamp which is fitted over the strings at the bridge, is often used on the violin and viola. It changes the tone color and produces a hollow, veiled sound.

---

[4] For a detailed discussion of this subject see Murphy, *ibid.*

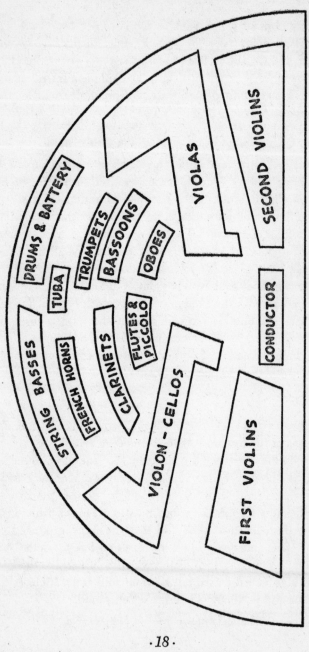

DIAGRAM 1. Seating Arrangement for Symphony Orchestra.

The Violin. The violin (Figure 1) has the highest pitch of all the stringed instruments. It is comparable to the soprano voice. The variety of tone color is almost infinite, and many special effects are possible. The most lyrical melodies are usually played on the violin, but the most rapid and intricate passages are equally feasible on this instrument. Among the special effects of the violin are playing two notes at once (double stopping), bouncing the bow on the strings (saltando), plucking the strings with the finger (pizzicato), and playing with the wooden part of the bow (col legno). In the orchestra the violins are divided into two sections which are seated on opposite sides of the concert platform and which play different parts. There are usually about sixteen players in each section.

The Viola. The viola (Figure 2) is slightly larger than the violin and produces a lower, mellower tone. It is comparable to the alto voice. All the special effects of the violin are possible on the viola. There are from ten to twelve violas in the modern symphony orchestra.

The Violoncello. The violoncello (Figure 3) is a still larger instrument that is held between the knees of the player. It is comparable to the tenor voice. The tone is rich and warm and the instrument has tremendous expressive possibilities. There are usually from eight to ten cellos in the symphony orchestra.

The String Bass. The string bass (Figure 4) is the largest of the string family, about six feet in height. The player stands, or sits on a high stool. The instrument has a deep, brusque tone which is employed to furnish a base for the harmonies above. It is seldom used for solo purposes. There are about ten string basses in the symphony orchestra.

WOOD WINDS

The wood-wind section of the orchestra is notable for varied and striking tone colors. Each of the instruments has a sharply differentiated quality, and many strange and alluring effects are possible. The four principal members of the wood-wind group are the flute, the oboe, the clarinet, and the bassoon. For each of these instruments there is another instrument closely related and similar in construction. The player of the principal instrument can usually perform on the related instrument. Some of these instruments are no longer made of wood but are still classified as wood winds.

The Flute. The flute (Figure 5), one of the oldest musical instruments, is suited for melodic work both florid and sustained. It is the most nimble of the wood winds and can execute rapid passages with ease. The tone of the flute is produced by blowing across a hole in the side of the instrument. The flute produces a birdlike tone and has a bright and piercing sound in its upper register. The lower register has a thick, misty tone. There are two or three flutists in the symphony orchestra.

The Piccolo. The piccolo is a small flute (Figure 5). Its name is derived from the Italian words *flauto piccolo,* meaning "little flute." It is about half as long as the flute and sounds an octave higher. It has a very shrill, glittering tone and is often called the "imp" of the orchestra. It is seldom given solo passages, but it is used in climaxes and for special effects, such as the moaning of the wind. There is usually one piccolo, which is played by one of the flutists, in the symphony orchestra.

The Oboe. The oboe (Figure 6) is a conical wooden pipe with a bell at one end. The tone is produced by blowing on a double reed. The oboe has a penetrating, nasal tone and is excellent for the expression of poignant melodies and for melodies of pastoral nature. There are usually three oboes in the symphony orchestra.

The English Horn. The English horn (Figure 7) is a large oboe. It is used primarily for solo passages where a melancholy, doleful quality is desired. There is usually one English horn, which is generally played by an oboist, in the symphony orchestra.

The Clarinet. The clarinet (Figure 8) is a cylindrical pipe with a small bell at the end. The tone is produced by blowing on a single reed. The clarinet is capable of great variety in tone color.

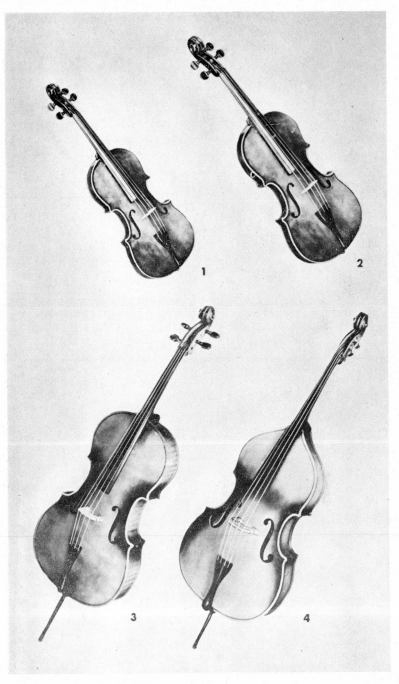

1. Violin   2. Viola   3. Violoncello   4. String Bass

(Courtesy of Pan-American Band Instruments.)

**5. Flute (above) and Piccolo 6. Oboe 7. English Horn 8. Clarinet 9. Bass Clarinet
10. Bassoon 11. Contra-Bassoon**

12. Trumpet 13. French Horn 14. Trombone 15. Tuba

(12., 13., 14.—C. G. Conn Ltd.; 15.—Fred. Gretsch Manufacturing Co.)

16. Guitar   17. Mandolin   18. Ukelele   19. Recorders—Soprano (left), Alto (center), and Tenor   20. Ocarina   21. Autoharp

(16., 17., 18., 19.—Carl Fischer Musical Instrument Co.; 20.—Fred. Gretsch Manufacturing Co.; 21.—Oscar Schmidt-International, Inc.)

The lower register has an oily, hollow, and ghostly tone; the upper register has a rich, pure tone. The clarinet can play rapid and intricate passages and has a tremendous range of dynamics. It is an ideal solo instrument. There are three clarinetists in the symphony orchestra.

The Bass Clarinet. The bass clarinet (Figure 9) is much larger than the clarinet and has a large bell at the end. It sounds an octave below the clarinet and forms a solid base for the wood-wind choir. It has a striking, rich, woody tone and is often used for solo passages of grave and portentous character. The orchestra has one bass clarinet which is played by a clarinetist.

The Bassoon. The bassoon (Figure 10) provides the bass for the wood-wind group. It has a long tube bent back upon itself, with the bell pointing upward. The tone is produced by blowing on a double reed. The bassoon has considerable agility and is capable of a terse, hollow tone as well as a lyrical, throaty tone of majestic and ardent color. There are three bassoons in the symphony orchestra.

The Contra-Bassoon. The contra-bassoon (Figure 11) has about sixteen feet of tubing doubled back on itself four times, with the bell pointing downward. It sounds an octave lower than the bassoon and corresponds to the string bass in the string section. It is seldom used for solo purposes, its normal function being to support the harmony of the orchestra. There is one contra-bassoon, which is played by a bassoonist, in the orchestra.

BRASSES

Each instrument in this group—trumpet, French horn, trombone, and tuba—has a cup-shaped mouthpiece. The player produces the tone by blowing into the mouthpiece and by the action of his taut lips against the mouthpiece. This sets the air in the instrument in vibration. On all these instruments, except the trombone, there is a series of valves which regulate the length of the column of air within the tube and determine the pitch. The trombone has a slide which is moved back and forth to change the length of the air column. The mute for brasses is a pear-shaped piece of wood or metal which is inserted in the bell of the instrument.

The Trumpet. The trumpet (Figure 12) is the soprano of the brass choir. Its crisp, brilliant tone is ideal for sharp climaxes and for martial effects. The mute produces a poetic tone of great beauty and warmth. When blown loudly, the muted trumpet produces a grotesque, vulgar tone. There are three trumpets in the symphony orchestra.

The French Horn. The most important of the brasses is the French horn (Figure 13). It is the alto of the brass section, and its tone has magnificent poetic and expressive powers. The horn is used in solo passages, and several horns often play four-part harmony to support melodies played by the strings and wood winds. The muted horn produces a soft, faraway effect which is lovely beyond description. There are from four to eight French horns in the symphony orchestra.

The Trombone. As was mentioned previously, the trombone (Figure 14) has a sliding tube which lengthens or shortens the column of air and determines the pitch. The trombone is capable of overwhelming volume and brilliance; when played softly, its tone gives the effect of majesty and nobility. There are three or four trombones in the symphony orchestra.

The Tuba. The tuba (Figure 15) has the deepest tone of the brass instruments. Its function is comparable to that of the string bass and contra-bassoon. It has a heavy, obtrusive tone. It is surprisingly flexible, but is seldom used for solo purposes. The orchestra has one tuba.

PERCUSSION INSTRUMENTS

The instruments in the percussion group, also known as the battery or "kitchen," are sounded by being struck. Their function is to emphasize the rhythm.

The Tympani. Chief among the percussion instruments are the tympani or kettle drums, large copper kettles covered with sheepskin or calfskin. They can be tuned, and the pitch is controlled by screws and foot pedals. The drums are struck with flexible felt-headed sticks. They are employed to build up orchestral volume for climaxes and suspense. There is usually one tympanist in the orchestra, and he has two or three instruments at hand in order to obtain all the necessary pitches.

Other Instruments. The other instruments in the percussion section are seldom used concurrently and usually can be handled by one player, except in compositions in which the rhythmic element predominates. The *snare drum* and *bass drum* are the same instruments which are used in military bands. The tone of the former is a brittle rattle and it is used for martial effects; the latter has a deep, reverberating sound. *Cymbals* are plates of metal which, when clashed together, produce a shattering dramatic effect. The *triangle,* a bent metal bar, is struck with a small metal rod and produces a sharp tinkling sound. The *gong* is a large disc of hammered brass which is struck with a felt-headed stick. An eerie effect is secured by striking it softly; when struck with force, it produces a portentous, metallic sound. The *xylophone* consists of a series of wooden bars which, when struck with wooden mallets, have an empty, clanking sound. This instrument has a great deal of agility and serves well in short, rapid passages.[5]

STYLE

There are many facets to the question of style in music. The term itself is subject to many interpretations and has varied connotations. It is often used in relation to the texture of music, or the way music is written, in which case the style may be polyphonic or homophonic. It is also used in relation to the manner in which the composer expresses himself in his music, in which case the style may be classic or romantic. The present discussion is limited to these two aspects of style.

---

[5] For a detailed discussion of tone color in relation to orchestral instruments see Edwin J. Stringham, *Listening to Music Creatively,* Chapter XI, "Tone Color in Music: The Orchestra" (New York: Prentice-Hall, Inc., 1946), pp. 131–157.

Polyphony and Homophony

The two basic styles in relation to the texture of music are poly-phony and homophony. The word *polyphony* is from the Greek *poly,* meaning many, and *phonus,* meaning voice. Polyphonic music literally is music with many voices. It is based on the art of counterpoint and is said to be contrapuntal. The term *counter-point* is derived from the Latin *punctus contra punctum,* point against point or note against note. In contrapuntal music several melodies or parts are combined simultaneously with harmonious results. A round is the simplest form of contrapuntal music.

From the thirteenth century on, many composers have created contrapuntal music. The culmination of this style occurred in the sixteenth century with the works of Giovanni Pierluigi Palestrina (1524–1594), Orlando di Lasso (1532–1594), and Tomás Luis de Victoria (1540–1608). For use in the service of the Catholic Church, these composers wrote glorious masses and motets which represent the height of achievement in the art of counterpoint for voices.

Johann Sebastian Bach (1685–1750) was the last and the greatest of the polyphonic masters. His fugues, oratorios, masses, and chorales are at the summit of the contrapuntal art. When a melody is tossed from one instrument to another in a symphonic work, it is the result of contrapuntal treatment. Much contem-porary music is essentially contrapuntal and has a great deal in common with the music of Bach.

The word *homophony* is from the Greek *homo,* meaning same, and *phonus,* meaning voice. Homophonic music literally is music with one voice. It has a background of chords and is based on harmony. There is usually a single melody supported by chords which move in blocks of combined parts. Homophonic music is conceived and constructed vertically in contrast with the hori-zontal construction of polyphonic music.

The music of the late eighteenth and nineteenth centuries is predominantly homophonic. Nevertheless, composers in these centuries deliberately combined the two styles, as in the oratorios of Haydn and Mozart and the works of Beethoven, Brahms, and Franck.

Classicism and Romanticism

The two basic styles in relation to manner of expression are classicism and romanticism. All music is an expression of human emotion, but the means and style of that expression vary. In classic music the composer seeks to express the universal aspects of human emotion. He concerns himself not only with what he wants to say, but also with perfecting the manner in which he says it— with form as well as content. The work of the classic composer is notable for its simplicity, clarity, and restraint. He avoids bizarre and unusual effects. He disciplines himself to work within an established framework. He is progressive, but not radical. Tradition is important to him. He seeks to bring the old tradition to a higher level, but seldom strikes out on new or different paths. He is a master technician.

In romantic music the composer seeks to express his own emotion rather than universal emotion. He looks at the world about him and expresses his own ideas and reactions to it. His outlook is subjective. His world is not rational and well ordered; it is a dream world, full of fantasy and fiction. His music is imaginative and sentimental. He is a radical; he rebels against the established order. Tradition and form are not sacred to him. Form is his servant and is subservient to his need for emotional expression. He strikes out in new paths and secures unusual and picturesque effects.

Most music contains both classic and romantic elements. The classic elements predominate in the music of the eighteenth century. Josef Haydn (1732–1809) and Wolfgang Amadeus Mozart (1756–1791) are generally considered representatives of the classic period, but there are romantic elements in the music of both and particularly in the music of Mozart.

During the early part of the nineteenth century the romantic elements gradually gained ascendancy. Ludwig van Beethoven (1770–1827) and Franz Schubert (1797–1828) form the bridge between classicism and romanticism. Romanticism in all the arts came into full flower during the middle of the nineteenth century. Composers of the romantic period include Wagner, Liszt, Brahms, Grieg, Dvořák, Franck, Gounod, Bizet, Verdi, Puccini, and Mac-Dowell.

TYPES OF COMPOSITIONS

Composers have developed and employed many different types of compositions as vehicles of expression. Some compositions are short and simple; others, long and complex. There is great variation in the media of performance. Some compositions are for voices, some for instruments, and others for combined voices and instruments. A composition may involve a single performer, a small ensemble, or a large ensemble with the participants numbered in the hundreds.

The principal vocal forms are the art song, the opera, and the oratorio. Instrumental forms include the sonata, the symphonic poem, and numerous smaller forms.

Instrumental music may be pure music or program music, and occasionally elements of both are found in a single composition. The distinction between pure music and program music is difficult to define and is often subtle. Every composer has something to say in his music and all music has meaning for the listener. If music has no literary or pictorial connection or connotation, it is considered pure music. The symphonies of Mozart and Haydn are examples of this. Program music fulfills a representational function. It may be descriptive or narrative and has a literary or pictorial connotation. Program music had its greatest development during the romantic period of the nineteenth century. The *Romeo and Juliet Overture* by Tschaikowski, the *Alpine Symphony* by Strauss, and *Peter and the Wolf* by Prokofieff are familiar examples of program music.

A short description and discussion of the most usual types of compositions which have had great significance in the development of music as an expressive art follows. They include the art song, ballet music, chamber music, the opera, the oratorio, the sonata, and the symphonic poem.

The Art Song

The art song has elements in common with the folk song. Both forms make use of that most personal of expressive media, the human voice and both treat subjects close to the human heart. However, there are many differences between the two forms. The words of the art song are usually lyric verse of the highest quality, while simple folk poems supply the words of a folk song. The art song most often is "through composed," that is, the song follows the poem throughout, while the folk song is strophic in structure, that is, the melody is repeated for each stanza of the poem. In the art song there is a perfect blending of the music and the text and the accompaniment is an integral part of the song. The undulations of the melody coincide with the rise and fall of emotion in the text. The composer expresses the spirit and the message of the poetry in music.

Although earlier composers such as Haydn, Henry Purcell (1658–1695), and Beethoven wrote songs for solo voices, it was the great German song writers of the nineteenth century who established the art song as a genuine art form. Schubert inaugurated this golden age of song and remains the first and foremost master of the form. He was inspired by the lyrics of Schiller, Goethe, and other great German poets and wrote nearly six hundred songs. Outstanding among them are *Der Erlkönig* (*The Erl King*), *The Hedge Rose, Die Allmacht* (*The Omnipotence*), *Der Tod und das Mädchen* (*Death and the Maiden*), and *Who Is Sylvia?*

Another great German song composer was Robert Schumann (1810–1856), who was particularly inspired by the poems of Heine. Among his finest songs are *Ich Grolle Nicht* (*I'll Not Complain*) and *Die Beiden Grenadiere* (*The Two Grenadiers*).

The third of the master composers in the German song tradition was Johannes Brahms (1833–1897). There is exquisite passion, fervor, and intensity in his songs. They show the influence of folk music and are often strophic in form. Among his splendid songs are *Sapphische Ode* (*Sapphic Ode*), *Die Mainacht* (*May Night*) and *Der Schmied* (*The Blacksmith*).

Other German composers, such as Robert Franz (1815–1892), Hugo Wolf (1860–1903), and Richard Strauss (1864–1949) continued the cultivation of the art song. In France the art song came into its own in the latter part of the nineteenth century. Outstanding French song composers include César Franck (1822–1890), Gabriel Fauré (1845–1924), Henri Duparc (1848–1933), and Claude Debussy (1862–1918). Edward Grieg (1843–1907), Norwegian, and Peter I. Tschaikowski (1840–1893), Russian, also excelled in this genre.

Ballet Music

Ballet music usually is highly rhythmic, melodious, dramatic, yet simple in form. During the nineteenth century the principal source of ballet music was opera or the incidental music for other dramatic performances. Ballet dances have been composed for Debussy's *L'Après-midi d'un faune* (*Afternoon of a Faun*) and Rimsky-Korsakoff's *Scheherazade*, although they were originally composed as concert pieces. Gradually the ballet established itself as an independent art form, and the need arose for music specifically designed for use in ballet.

Much of this music, composed especially for ballet, has become a part of the concert literature. Examples are Stravinsky's *Le Sacre du Printemps* (*The Rites of Spring*) and *L'Oiseau de feu* (*The Firebird*); Ravel's *Mother Goose Suite* and *Boléro;* Aaron Copland's *Billy the Kid* and *Rodeo;* Walter Piston's *The Incredible Flutist;* and Tschaikowski's *Swan Lake* and *Sleeping Beauty.*

Chamber Music

The original meaning of the term "chamber music" was music designed and best suited for performance in a drawing room or a private chamber. Today, chamber music is usually performed by a small group of players in a small concert hall. The intimacy of chamber music and its limited range of dynamics make it ideal music to play on recordings in one's own living room.

The most common form of chamber music is the string quartet, which is composed of first violin, second violin, viola, and cello. To this basic unit a fifth instrument of different quality, such as a piano or a clarinet, is often added to form a quintet. Other combinations are the piano trio, which consists of a piano, violin, and cello, and groups of various sizes from three to eight or nine instruments of different types. The chamber orchestra usually is composed of about twenty players. Occasionally voices are blended with the instruments.

Chamber music is the purest of pure music. It lacks the sonority and range of color and dynamics of the orchestral compositions, but it has a purity of tone and a perfection of blend that compensate for this lack. In listening to chamber music a person can follow each instrument as it assumes the responsibility for carrying the melody and can savor the mingling of the entwining parts. All the instruments are of nearly equal importance, and no instrument serves solely as an accompaniment to a solo instrument.

The inexperienced listener may at first find chamber music rather lusterless and dry, but, if he continues to listen, he will discover its charm and find the experience a most satisfying one.

The chamber music of Beethoven is generally conceded to be the most profound in this genre. Other chamber music well worth the listening includes that of Mozart, Schubert, Brahms, Tschaikowsky, Dvořák, and Ravel.

The Opera

Opera is a synthesis of many arts. It involves painting, drama, costuming, dancing, acting, and, of course, music—an orchestra, soloists, choruses, and ensembles. All these elements are joined to tell a story.

Opera in some form has been a part of the culture of most of the civilizations of the world. The Greeks and Romans had elaborate dramas which combined song and dance. In the Middle Ages there were both sacred and secular musical plays. Oriental civilizations—Indian, Chinese, Javanese, Japanese, and Persian —have all cultivated forms of expression closely akin to opera.

There are two basic types of opera or music drama: grand opera and comic opera or operetta. The musical comedy of the present day grew out of the latter type.

GRAND OPERA

Grand opera is generally of tragic character and mood. It is sung throughout; the dialogue is carried on by musical declamation called *recitative*. Grand opera is often based on historical or mythological characters or events and involves an extravagant use of soloists, chorus, dancers, scenery, and costumes.

The three great centers of grand opera are Italy, France, and Germany. Italian opera is characterized by its tendency to subordinate the dramatic aspects of the opera to vocalism. It is dominated by arias or solos sung by the principal characters. The arias are tuneful and melodious and allow for impressive displays of vocal technique. There are pauses for applause at the end of each aria. In early Italian opera the arias often had little or nothing to do with the flow of the dramatic action. If a well-known singer were singing a role, the composer would sometimes write an extra aria and insert it in the opera in order to please him. At the beginning of the nineteenth century there was a trend toward a better combination of the dramatic and vocal aspects in Italian opera. Gioacchino Rossini (1792–1868) and Gaetano Donizetti (1797–

1848) were influential in this trend. Giuseppe Verdi (1813–1901) was the greatest of the Italian operatic composers. He succeeded in combining the Italian vocal tradition with dramatic and musical expressiveness. His arias are almost always pertinent to the drama. *Rigoletto* and *La Traviata* remain a fresh and ever-popular part of the operatic repertory of the present day. His finest works are those written in his maturity: *Aïda, Otello,* and *Falstaff.* The most successful Italian operatic composer since Verdi is Giacomo Puccini (1858–1924), the composer of *La Bohème, La Tosca,* and *Madame Butterfly.*

The origin of French opera lies in the ballet, though it also shows the influence of the French classic theater. The most important contribution of France to operatic literature is the *drame lyrique* in which the musical declamation is adapted to the French language and there is a lyric quality to the music. Works in this category are *Faust* by Charles Gounod (1819–1893), *Manon* by Jules Massenet (1842–1912), *Carmen* by Georges Bizet (1838–1875), *Louise* by Gustaf Charpentier (1860–   ), and *Pelléas and Mélisande* by Claude Debussy (1862–1918).

The hallmark of German opera is the orchestra, which is used for dramatic effect rather than as mere accompaniment to the singing. Mozart is the earliest German opera composer who remains in today's repertory. His *Don Giovanni* ranks as one of the finest music dramas ever written. It combines the vocal tradition of Italian opera and the orchestral tradition of the German. Richard Wagner (1813–1883) stands at the apogee of German opera. The Wagnerian orchestra provides a web of harmony which sets the stage for the dramatic action. Out of this rich orchestral context the vocal line arises in what Wagner called "continuous melodies," which replace the arias of Italian opera. The choruses, ensembles, and ballets grow out of the dramatic action. The pace of Wagnerian operas is slower than that of Italian and French operas. Wagner's early period is represented by *Der Fliegende Holländer* (*The Flying Dutchman*), in which the principles of Italian opera are apparent. His later works include *Lohengrin, Tannhäuser, Die*

Meistersinger, and *The Ring,* a cycle of four operas composed of *Das Rheingold, Die Walküre, Siegfried,* and *Die Götterdämmerung.* It was in *Tristan und Isolde* and *Parsifal* that Wagner reached the most laudable heights of German music drama.

COMIC OPERA

Comic opera or operetta is known in France as *opera bouffe,* in Italy as *opera buffa,* and in Germany as *singspiel* (song-play). Comic opera is a popular kind of opera, the subject of which is close to the life of the people. It is a musical play in which the songs and dances are usually mingled with spoken dialogue. The masterpiece of this genre is Mozart's *Marriage of Figaro.* Other outstanding early examples are *La Serva Padrona* by Pergolesi, *The Magic Flute* by Mozart, and *The Barber of Seville* by Rossini. The operettas of Gilbert and Sullivan fall into this category as do Victor Herbert's *Fortune Teller* and *Mlle. Modiste,* Rudolph Friml's *Rose Marie,* Sigmund Romberg's *Blossom Time,* and George Gershwin's *Porgy and Bess.*

The Oratorio

An oratorio is a musical setting of a dramatic text sung by soloists and chorus accompanied by an orchestra. The subject is usually sacred or spiritual. Opera and oratorio had a common origin, and for many years oratorios were acted out with scenery and costumes. With the introduction of a narrator, dramatic action disappeared from the oratorio. Today, opera and oratorio are separate and distinct forms. An oratorio differs from a mass in that a mass is designed to serve as a part of the church service, while the oratorio is performed at times other than during the service. The chorus is the dominant feature of an oratorio and the major means of securing dramatic effect. Composers of all periods have written oratorios. *The Messiah* by George Frederick Handel (1685–1759) is undoubtedly the best known of the oratorios. Among Handel's other works in this form are *Saul, Judas Maccabeus,* and *Israel in Egypt.* Bach's oratorios are concerned with the Passions of Christ. He wrote the *St. Matthew Passion,* the *St. John Passion,* and the *St. Luke Passion,* as well as *The Christmas Oratorio.*

The finest oratorios of the classic period are *The Creation* and *The Seasons* by Haydn. The great oratorio writer of the romantic period was Felix Mendelssohn (1809–1847), whose *Elijah* and *St. Paul* rank with *The Messiah* and *The Creation* as the most profound and exalted of sacred music. Recently composed oratorios include William Walton's *Belshazzar's Feast,* Frederick Delius' *The Mass of Life,* Honegger's *King David* and *Penitential Psalm,* Horatio Parker's *Hora Novissima,* and D'Indy's *Legend of St. Christopher.*

The Sonata

The most important of the forms of pure music is the *sonata.* The term "sonata" comes from *sonare,* to sound. A sonata is an extended instrumental composition which usually has three or four movements. There are solo sonatas for piano, violin, flute, cello, organ, and other instruments; and sonatas for any two instruments, such as violin and piano. A sonata for three instruments is a *trio* sonata; for four instruments, a *quartet;* and for five instruments, a *quintet.* If the sonata is written for a solo instrument and orchestra, it is called a *concerto,* as, for example, a violin concerto or a piano concerto. If a full orchestra plays a sonata it is called a *symphony.*

The first and last movements of a sonata are usually fast in tempo and complex in design. They are likely to be profound in mood and highly developed. The second movement is usually slow in tempo and lyric in character. The third movement, ordinarily a minuet or scherzo, is the dance movement with a spirited rhythm and a gay lilting character. The order of the movements is sometimes changed, particularly in the romantic sonata. Most instrumental composers have written sonatas for the different media. The sonata remains the dominant form of pure music.

The Symphonic Poem

The symphonic poem or tone poem, an important form of program music, developed out of the romantic period. It occupies the same relative position in program music that the sonata has in pure music. At one time there was a difference between a symphonic poem and a tone poem, but today the terms are practically interchangeable. This form may be descriptive or narrative; it describes a mood or a scene or tells a story. The symphonic poem is usually in one movement and its design is necessarily flexible and free. Richard Strauss excelled in this form. Among his finest works are *Till Eulenspiegel's Merry Pranks, Don Juan,* and *Death and Transfiguration.* Other outstanding symphonic poems are Liszt's *Les Preludes* (*Symphonic Poem No. 3*), Saint-Saens' *Danse Macabre,* Schönberg's *Transfigured Night,* Respighi's *The Pines of Rome* and *The Fountains of Rome,* Moussorgsky's *Night on Bald Mountain,* Dukas' *Sorcerer's Apprentice,* and Gershwin's *An American in Paris.*

OPPORTUNITIES TO LISTEN TO MUSIC

The average person has greater opportunities for hearing fine music in the United States today than ever before in the history of the world. At one time listening to music was one of the privileges of the wealthy. Today, everyone, regardless of his financial circumstances, can hear the best of music at concerts and recitals, on the radio, on television, and through the medium of recordings.

Concerts and Recitals

Concerts and recitals take place in every community in the country. The large cities have always had an active music season extending from September to May. Most of the larger cities have symphony orchestras which give one or more concerts each week during the season, often with outstanding artists as soloists. Several cities have opera companies and chamber music groups which offer regular performances. In addition, there are numerous recitals by established artists and by young artists striving to establish themselves. When these professional performances are combined with countless performances by amateur singers, instrumentalists, choral groups, and orchestras, and with the music programs of the schools and churches, the result is a musical environment so rich and full that a person has difficulty in deciding what to hear and what to miss.

In recent years many smaller cities and towns have developed fine orchestras and opera companies, and the community concert movement has brought them fine recitalists. The music programs of the colleges, schools, churches, and other organizations further enrich the musical environment and actually are a more important factor in these towns than in the large cities.

There are several advantages to hearing music at a concert or recital. The listener has both visual and auditory contact which results in a sense of direct communication with the artist. One can enjoy the full force of the artist's personality and develop a feeling of familiarity with him. There is a quality of immediacy, of being on the spot, in hearing an artist in person, and the listener feels that he is a participant in the performance. Furthermore, if the recital hall has good acoustics, he hears the music in all of its tonal richness. Being part of an audience for a fine recital gives most people thrilling satisfaction.

Music on the Radio

A person who plans his radio listening carefully can hear a great deal of fine music. The Saturday afternoon broadcasts of the Metropolitan Opera Association are outstanding. A person can increase his understanding and enjoyment of these broadcasts by subscribing to *The Opera News*, published by the Metropolitan Opera Guild, 654 Madison Avenue, New York 21, New York. This excellent magazine, published weekly during the opera season, gives complete information about the opera to be broadcast that week. It includes the story of the opera, background material about the composer and the artists who are singing, reviews of operatic recordings, and other pertinent and interesting data. Other fine broadcasts are Sunday afternoon concerts by the New York Philharmonic Society, the rehearsals of the Boston Symphony, the Firestone Hour, and the Telephone Hour. In many communities there are frequency modulation stations which offer programs made up exclusively of classical music. Some of the stations publish program guides, which list all the compositions to be played during the month, as an aid in planning a listening schedule.

Music on Television

Television is the infant of the entertainment and communication industry. To date, the emphasis has been upon variety shows and comedy, but there are a few good music programs. Among them are the Firestone Hour and an occasional opera telecast. Television viewers can play an important part in increasing the number of music programs by informing the broadcasters of their desires. Television has tremendous possibilities as a medium for hearing music. It combines many of the advantages of concerts and recitals with those of radio broadcasts.

Music on Recordings

More and better music is available on recordings today than ever before. Recent advances in recording techniques and equipment have resulted in recordings of a quality never before equalled. There is active competition among recording companies, and the entire industry is bending every effort to improve the quality of releases. Although there are a few regrettable gaps in recorded literature, the entrance of new domestic concerns and foreign companies into the field is resulting in a constant expansion of the range of choice.

In many respects recordings provide the medium *par excellence* for listening to music. The listener need not leave his own home to listen to them. He can make his own choice and plan his own program of listening. He can hear a composition, or a part of it, as many times as he wishes. He can hear what he wants to hear when he wants to hear it. He is a free agent and completely independent in his listening. This independence brings with it problems in selection and care of recordings. These problems are the concern of the next chapter.

CHAPTER THREE

THE RECREATION LEADER AND THE LISTENING PROGRAM

A good listening program in organized recreation takes into account the needs and desires of those whom it serves. The responsibility for developing and implementing the program rests with the recreation leader. If he has some knowledge of music, and the program is small, he may handle it himself. The listening area, unlike some areas of the music program, can be directed by a person who has a minimum of musical skill. Any intelligent person with enthusiasm for music can accomplish a great deal in developing the listening program. In a large program the leader needs the assistance of one or more persons with special ability and knowledge in music, particularly if classes in music appreciation are part of the offering. These assistants may be full- or part-time employees or volunteer workers.

THE FUNCTIONS OF THE RECREATION LEADER

The functions of the recreation leader will be different in each situation. In developing the listening program, he should take into account his own competencies and those of his co-workers and should determine the desires of those participating in the program. Suggestions for appropriate functions of the leader follow:

1. *Providing necessary facilities and equipment.* The facilities and equipment necessary depend upon the nature and extent of

the listening program, but, in order to have a growing program, the leader must anticipate developments and always be ready for any extension of the program. The facilities should care for the needs of both groups and individuals. One or more rooms with good acoustics are necessary for listening by groups. It is desirable that one room be equipped with comfortable chairs, a good phonograph, radio, and television set, or a combination of these, and that the recording library be close by. In addition, provision should be made for listening by individuals, by way of several small sound-proof rooms equipped with record players. Another possibility is to secure a listening table equipped with several turntables and individual ear phones.

2. *Planning programs of recorded music.* In many situations, informal programs of recorded music form an appropriate and important part of the recreation program. Many schools, camps, industrial groups, and other organizations have programs on a regular schedule. They may occur during the lunch hour, in the evening, or during regular breaks in the schedule of work or study.

These programs are recreational and only incidentally educational. This means that there need be no discussion or instruction. All that is necessary is to provide a quiet, comfortable setting for enjoyable listening. It is essential that the person responsible for the programs use the best available phonograph and that he plan each program so that there will be variety in the music played. The listeners should be allowed to come and go at will, the only restriction being that they not disturb the rest of the group. It is important that there be an opportunity for the listeners to request compositions and that each program be posted conspicuously and well in advance. In addition, the title of the composition, the name of the composer, and the names of the principal performing artists should be written on a blackboard or in some other way revealed to the group before each composition is played.

3. *Organizing music appreciation classes.* The music appreciation course has both recreational and educational implications. The purpose of such a course is to give the participants experience

in directed listening and to enhance their enjoyment of music by providing information about music and musicians. The emphasis, however, is properly placed on listening and not on information. There needs to be continuity from one session to the next, but each session should be reasonably complete within itself so that the course will be meaningful to those who cannot attend regularly.

The principal qualifications for the person directing a course in appreciation are a broad knowledge of music literature, enthusiasm for music, and willingness to make careful preparation for each session. It is often feasible to secure the services of a local musician or music educator.

There are fine, available books on music appreciation. Although most of them are designed for use in the public schools or in colleges, those listed below are recommended for use in recreation programs:

ADLER, LAWRENCE. *New Values in Music Appreciation.* New York: Roerich Museum Press, 1935.

FINNEY, THEODORE MITCHELL. *Hearing Music.* New York: Harper and Brothers, 1941.

MURPHY, HOWARD A. *Form in Music for the Listener.* Camden, N.J.: RCA Victor, 1948.

McGEHEE, THOMASINE C. *People and Music* (New Edition). New York: Allyn and Bacon, 1939.

STRINGHAM, EDWIN S. *Listening to Music Creatively.* New York: Prentice-Hall, Inc., 1946.

4. *Arranging concerts and recitals.* Concerts and recitals serve a dual purpose: they give pleasure to the audience and they give the performers an opportunity to be heard. Live performances have a special appeal for most people and offer a welcome change from listening to programs that are mechanically reproduced. In every community, there are soloists, choral groups, and instrumental groups who desire to appear in public and who welcome the opportunity to do so. The recreation leader must inform himself about the musical resources of the community and take full advantage of them in presenting concerts and recitals.

5. *Publicizing music programs that take place in the community.* Many music programs are given without the awareness of the people in the community. There are excellent programs on radio and television. Schools, churches, and commercial enterprises constantly sponsor worth-while concerts and recitals. The recreation leader should secure information about the musical events that are taking place in the community and disseminate the information by means of announcements, posters, and notices on bulletin boards. He may also set up a ticket bureau to help people in securing tickets.

6. *Setting up a record library and offering records for loan or rental.* Availability of recordings is an important factor in enriching musical experience and in developing an interest in music. Many people cannot afford to purchase all the recordings they would like to hear. Others may wish to hear and assess a recording before purchasing it. The recreation leader may give assistance in both these respects by lending or renting recordings on a short-term basis.

The selection and maintenance of recordings and recording equipment are basic problems in developing the listening program. The remainder of the chapter is concerned with the solution of these problems.

BUILDING A RECORD LIBRARY

The choice of recordings for a library is a personal matter, and the proper selection necessarily and rightly differs with each person or group of people. A person's choice of recordings depends upon his background and taste. Choosing one's own recordings can be an exciting adventure and the pleasure of doing so should not be denied to anyone. Although many attempts have been made, it is next to impossible, and ultimately futile, to select a basic library that will suit exactly the needs and tastes of any considerable number of people.

A few general guides may help to assure a good choice from the vast store of available recorded music. It is also possible and desirable to suggest recordings in different forms and different media that will aid the novice listener in becoming acquainted with and interested in music. After this initial acquaintance and interest has been developed, the intelligent person will acquire taste, discrimination, and judgment in selecting his own recordings.

Guides for Selection of Recordings

One should choose, at first, a few recordings of music which are known and liked and a few which are unfamiliar. The best point of departure in broadening a person's musical experience is his present level of comprehension and appreciation. Everyone has a few favorite compositions which appeal to him and which he would like to hear frequently. These should make up the bulk of the first recordings he purchases. On the other hand, a few recordings of unfamiliar music lend variety to his listening and serve to expand his acquaintance with music.

One should choose, at first, recordings of music containing elements that have an immediate appeal. For many people, particularly those who know little about music, listening to program music has proved to be an effective beginning. Program music is dramatic and stirring. Its descriptive or narrative character has a vivid appeal for the inexperienced listener. If he knows the program, he has a tangible factor on which to focus his attention. The *Romeo and Juliet Overture* by Tschaikowski, for example, stirs and thrills the listener as it portrays the familiar story.

Music in which rhythm is the dominant element is excellent for introducing a person to the pleasure of listening to music. Responsiveness to rhythm is universal. Rhythm appeals to the sensuous nature and is tremendously exciting. Ravel's *Boléro*, Brahms' *Hungarian Dances*, and Dvořák's *Slavonic Dances* are examples of highly rhythmic music.

Music with lovely, singable melodies is also fine for the novice listener. The melody is tangible, something he can take to his heart, savor, and enjoy both while listening and at other times. Mozart's *Eine Kleine Nachtmusik* and the Grieg *A Minor Concerto* are examples of music with fascinating melodies.

It is desirable to develop an ever-expanding horizon in musical experience. It is unfortunate to become overspecialized in one's listening. A listener who becomes so entranced with Beethoven that he fails to hear Tschaikowski, Haydn, or Hindemith is not partaking of a balanced musical fare. One would consider a constant diet of one food unacceptable; an unbalanced and unchanging musical diet is no better. One learns to know and love music only by experiencing it.

Recordings should have variety as to type and period of music, composer, medium of performance, and performer. The music of every period, every type, every composer, and for every medium has its own particular charm and worth. To neglect any segment of music literature means a loss in pleasure and breadth of background. No conductor, vocalist, or other artist excels in all types of music. Each artist has his own forte in which he does his finest work.

A record library should be limited to such size as will permit listening to the greater portion of it within a reasonable period of time. Music is to be heard and should not merely fill space in a record cabinet. A recording is usually an unwise expenditure if there is no reasonable expectancy of listening to it occasionally.

Moreover, a record library should be assembled slowly and carefully. A hastily chosen recording is often disappointing. Too rapid acquisition prevents a person from enjoying his recordings to the fullest possible extent. It is preferable for the listener and his library to grow together.

It is wise to hear all the available performances of the same work before selecting a recording. There are usually several different recordings of a given work. One company may have more than one release, and several companies probably have it in their catalogues. It is a sound plan to consult the opinions of reputable music critics on the relative merits of different performances before listening to them. The final judgment, however, should be that of the purchaser; he is the one to be pleased. Critics are, after all, not infallible, and one's taste may justly differ from theirs.

It should be ascertained that performances on recordings are in their original setting and that they conform to the intentions of the composer. For some obscure reason, many recordings have been released in arrangements or adaptations that do serious violence to the composer's intentions. They may be instrumental settings of vocal works, or, even worse, vocal arrangements of instrumental compositions. Most of them are cheap and deplorable. The outstanding exception is found in some of the orchestral transcriptions of organ or piano compositions, many of which are made with considerable taste and quite effectively.

Only recordings that are mechanically perfect should be bought. There is considerable variation in the quality of reproduction in recordings. Some processes of recording are superior to others, and some recording materials have advantages over others. Therefore the quality of the recording will vary from company to company, within the releases of the same company, and even in different pressings of the same recording. In addition, recordings are occasionally damaged in storage or transit. The only sure protection for the record buyer is to hear each recording and to inspect each disc for evidence of scratches, warping, cracks, and off-center pressing.

Recordings for Adults

If one is building a record library for himself or for an organization, the specific list of suggested recordings provided here may be helpful.

The list is organized by these types of compositions, in alphabetical order: art songs, ballet music, chamber music, choral music, concertos, opera (vocal and orchestral selections), orchestral compositions (miscellaneous), symphonies, symphonic poems, overtures (other than operatic), piano music, and sacred songs. For each composition, the particular recorded version that appeals most to the author is cited. In each description, the name of the principal performing artist or artists, the name of the orchestra, the name of the recording company, the catalogue number, and the number and size of the recording is given. Unless otherwise noted, the recordings cited here are of the standard 78-revolutions-per-minute, but many of the recordings are available on long-playing records as well.

All the recordings cited are currently available. There is considerable instability in recording catalogues, and issues are replaced or withdrawn from time to time, with the result that occasionally it is difficult to secure a particular recording. However, all the compositions listed are almost certain to be available in a satisfactory recorded performance.

Compositions especially appropriate for the inexperienced listener are marked with an asterisk.

ART SONGS

Beethoven, *An die Ferne Geliebte,* opus 98—Gerhard Hüsch, baritone—Victor 12246–7, two 10″.

Brahms, *Zigeunerlieder*—Lotte Lehmann, soprano—Victor Set 1188, two 10″.

Grieg, *Et Håb, Der Gynger en-Baad paa Bölge, Im Kahne, Ein Schwan, Ein Traum*—Kirsten Flagstad, soprano—Victor Set 342, five 10″.

Haydn, *°She Never Told Her Love, My Mother Bids Me Bind My Hair*—Marian Anderson, contralto—Victor 10–1199, one 10″.

Mozart, *Das Veilchen*—Elizabeth Schumann, soprano—His Master's Voice DA 1854, one 10″.

Schubert, *°Ave Maria*—Marian Anderson, contralto—Victor 14210, one 12″.

Der Erlkönig—Alexander Kipnis, baritone—Victor 15825, one 12″.

Der Tod und das Mädchen—Marian Anderson, contralto—Victor 1862, one 10″.

°Who Is Sylvia?—Jussi Bjoerling, tenor—Victor 12725, one 12″.

Schumann, *°Alte Laute* and *Du Bist wie eine Blume*—Lotte Lehmann, soprano—Victor Set 419, six 10″.

Die Lotosblume and *Widmung*—Herbert Janssen, baritone—Victor 1931, one 10″.

Strauss, Richard, *Allerseelen, Morgen, Ständchen* and *Zueignung*—Lotte Lehmann, soprano—Columbia Set X 270, two 10″.

Tschaikowski, *None but the Lonely Heart*—Leonard Warren, baritone—Victor 10-1406, one 10″.

Williams, Vaughan, *Silent Noon*—Roy Henderson, bass—English Decca M 583, one 10″.

BALLET MUSIC

Copland, *Appalachian Spring*—Serge Koussevitsky and the Boston Symphony Orchestra—Victor Set 1046, one 12″.

de Falla, *Ritual Fire Dance*—Arthur Fiedler and the Boston "Pops" Orchestra—Victor 12160, one 12″.

Delibes, *Excerpts from the Coppélia Ballet Suite*—Constant Lambert and the Royal Opera House Orchestra—Columbia Set 775, four 12″.

Khachaturian, *Sabre Dance* from *Gayne Ballet Suite No. 1* and *Waltz* from *Masquerade*—Artur Rodzinsky and the Chicago Symphony Orchestra—Victor 12-0209, one 12″.

Offenbach, *Gaieté Parisienne*—Efrem Kurtz and the London Philharmonic Orchestra—Columbia Set X 115, two 12″.

Piston, *The Incredible Flutist*—Arthur Fiedler and the Boston "Pops" Orchestra—Victor Set 621, two 12″.

Ravel, *Daphnis and Chloé Suite No. 1*—Pierre Monteux and the San Francisco Symphony Orchestra—Victor Set 1143, four 12″.

Rimsky-Korsakoff, *Scheherazade*—Eugene Ormandy and the Philadelphia Orchestra—Columbia Set 772, five 12″.

Schönberg, *Verklaerte Nacht* (*Pillar of Fire*)—Vladimir Golschmann and the St. Louis Symphony Orchestra—Victor Set 1005, five 12″.

Shostakovitch, *Polka* from *L'Âge d'Or*—Efrem Kurtz and the Philadelphia Orchestra—Columbia 7-3-101, one 7″.

Stravinsky, *Le Sacre du Printemps*—Pierre Monteux and the San Francisco Symphony Orchestra—Victor Set 1052, four 12″.

Tschaikowski, *Nutcracker Suite*—Eugene Goosens and the London Symphony Orchestra—Victor Set G 5, three 12″.

CHAMBER MUSIC

Beethoven, *String Quartet No. 6 in B Flat,* opus 18, No. 6—Budapest String Quartet—Columbia Set 754, three 12″.

String Quartet No. 14 in C-sharp Minor, opus 131—Budapest String Quartet—Columbia Set 429, five 12".

String Trio No. 2 in G, opus 9, No. 1—Pasquier Trio—Columbia Set 384, three 12".

Piano Trio No. 7 in B Flat, opus 97—Artur Rubinstein, Jascha Heifetz, and Emanuel Feuermann—Victor Set 949, five 12".

Brahms, *Quintet for Strings in F Major,* opus 88—Budapest String Quartet with Alfred Hobday, cello—Victor Set 466, three 12".

Dvorák, **Quartet in E Flat,* opus 51—Busch Quartet—Columbia Set 480, four 12".

Haydn, **String Quartet in G,* opus 54, No. 1—Budapest String Quartet—Victor Set 869, two 12".

Mozart, *String Quartet No. 17 in B Flat (Jagd)*—Budapest String Quartet—Victor Set 763, three 12".

*Quintet in G (Eine Kleine Nachtmusik), K 525—Pro Arte Quartet with Claude Hobday, string bass—Victor Set 428, two 12".

Serenade No. 10 in B Flat, K 361—Wilhelm Fürtwangler and an ensemble from the Vienna Philharmonic Orchestra—His Master's Voice DB 9226–30, five 12".

Schubert, *String Quartet in D Minor (Death and the Maiden)*—Philharmonia Quartet—English Columbia DX 1089–92, four 12".

CHORAL MUSIC

Bach, *Cantata No. 4 (Christ Lag im Todesbaden)*—Robert Shaw and the RCA Victor Chorale—Victor Set 1096, four 10".

Von Himmel Hoch—Trapp Family Choir—Victor 713, four 10".

Handel, **Behold the Lamb of God* from *The Messiah*—Sir Malcolm Sargent and the Royal Choral Society with the London Philharmonic Orchestra—Victor 11824, one 12".

*Hallelujah Chorus from *The Messiah*—Warwick Braithwaite and the Sadler's Wells Chorus and Orchestra—Victor 11–8670, one 12".

Mozart, *Ave Verum,* K 618—Strasbourg Cathedral Choir—Columbia 69488, one 12".

Victoria, *Kyrie: "Orbis Factor"*—Choir of Dijon Cathedral—Victor 71678, one 12".

Walton, *Belshazzar's Feast*—Composer conducting the Huddersfield Choral Society with the Liverpool Philharmonic Orchestra—Victor Set 974, five 12".

CONCERTOS

Beethoven, *Piano Concerto No. 1 in C,* opus 15—Artur Schnabel and the London Symphony Orchestra led by Sir Malcolm Sargent—Victor Set 158, five 12".

Brahms, *Piano Concerto in B Flat,* opus 83—Vladimir Horowitz and the NBC Symphony Orchestra led by Arturo Toscanini—Victor Set 740, six 12".

Violin Concerto in D, opus 77—Josef Szigetti and the Philadelphia Orchestra led by Eugene Ormandy—Columbia Set 603, five 12".

Franck, *Symphonic Variations*—Dame Myra Hess and the City of Birmingham Orchestra led by George Weldon—His Master's Voice C 3237-8, two 12".

Gershwin, *Piano Concerto in F*—Oscar Levant and the Philadelphia Orchestra led by André Kostelanetz—Columbia Set 512, four 12".

Grieg, *Piano Concerto in A Minor*—Artur Rubinstein and the Philadelphia Orchestra led by Eugene Ormandy—Victor Set 900, three 12".

Handel, *Oboe Concerto No. 1 in B Flat*—Leon Goosens and the London Philharmonic Orchestra led by Eugene Goosens—Victor 12605, one 12".

Haydn, *Harpsichord Concerto in D,* opus 21—Wanda Landowska and an orchestra led by Eugène Bigot—Victor Set 471, three 12".

Mendelssohn, *Piano Concerto No. 1 in G Minor*—Eileen Joyce and the London Symphony Orchestra led by Anatole Fistoulari—English Decca AK 1688-9, two 12".

Mozart, *Piano Concerto No. 21 in C,* K 467—Artur Schnabel and the London Symphony Orchestra led by Sir Malcolm Sargent—Victor Set 486, four 12".

Rachmaninoff, *Piano Concerto No. 1 in F-sharp Minor*—Composer and the Philadelphia Orchestra led by Eugene Ormandy—Victor Set 865, three 12".

Schumann, *Piano Concerto in A Minor*—Artur Rubinstein and the RCA Victor Orchestra led by William Steinberg—Victor Set 1176, four 12".

Tschaikowski, *Piano Concerto No. 1 in B-flat Minor*—Artur Rubinstein and the Minneapolis Symphony Orchestra led by Dimitri Mitropoulos—Victor Set 1159, four 12".

OPERA (Vocal Selections)

Bizet, *Toreador Song* from *Carmen*—Robert Merrill, baritone—Victor 11–2794, one 12″.

Donizetti, *Una furtiva lagrima* from *L'Elisir d'Amore*—Richard Crooks, tenor—Victor 15235, one 12″.

Handel, *Ombra mai fu* from *Serse*—Kathleen Ferrier, contralto—English Decca K 2135, one 12″.

Leoncavallo, *Prologue* to *Pagliacci*—Leonard Warren, baritone—Victor 11–9790, one 12″.

Mascagni, *Voi lo sapete* from *Cavalleria Rusticana*—Zinka Milanov, soprano—Victor 11–8927, one 12″.

Massenet, *Le Reve* from *Manon*—Jussi Bjoerling, tenor—Victor 12635, one 12″.

Offenbach, *Barcarolle* from *Tales of Hoffman*—Jennie Tourel, mezzo-soprano—Columbia Set X 299, two 12″.

Puccini, *Che gelida manina* from *La Bohème*—Jussi Bjoerling, tenor—Victor 12039, one 12″.

Mi chiamano Mimi from *La Bohème*—Bidù Sayão, soprano—Columbia 71320, one 12″.

Madame Butterfly (Excerpts)—Licia Albanese, soprano, James Melton, tenor, and Lucielle Browning, contralto—Victor Set 1068, three 12″.

Vissi d'arte from *Tosca*—Rose Bampton, soprano—Victor 11–8237, one 12″.

Purcell, *When I Am Laid in Earth* from *Dido and Aeneas*—Marian Anderson, contralto—Victor 17257, one 12″.

Rossini, *Una voce poco fa* from *The Barber of Seville*—Lily Pons, soprano—Victor 8870, one 12″.

Thomas, *Connais-tu le pays?* from *Mignon*—Risë Stevens, mezzo-soprano—Columbia 71192, one 12″.

Je suis Titania from *Mignon*—Lily Pons, soprano—Victor Set 702, three 12″.

Verdi, *Celeste Aïda* from *Aïda*—Jussi Bjoerling, tenor—Victor 12039, one 12″.

Ritorna vincitor from *Aïda*—Dusolina Giannini, soprano—Victor 9491, one 12″.

Eri tu from *Un Ballo in Maschera* and *Credo* from *Otello*—Leonard Warren, baritone—Victor 11–9292, one 12″.

La donna è mobile from *Rigoletto*—Jussi Bjoerling, tenor—Victor 4372, one 10″.

Ah! fors' è lui from *La Traviata*—Licia Albenese, soprano—Victor 11–9331, one 12".

Miserere from *Il Trovatore*—Jan Pierce, tenor, and Zinka Milanov, soprano—Victor 11–8782, one 12".

Wagner, Elsa's *Träume* from *Lohengrin*—Helen Traubel, soprano—Columbia 12321, one 12".

Immolation from *Götterdämmerung*—Helen Traubel and the NBC Symphony Orchestra—Victor Set 853, three 12".

Love Duet from *Tristan und Isolde*—Lauritz Melchior, tenor, and Kirsten Flagstad, soprano, with the San Francisco Symphony Orchestra—Victor Set 671, two 12".

OPERA (Orchestral selections)

Berlioz, *The Damnation of Faust* (Orchestral Excerpts)—Sir Thomas Beecham and the London Philharmonic Orchestra—Columbia Set X 94, two 12".

de Falla, *Dance No. 1 (Spanish Dance)* from *La Vida Breve*—Vladimir Goltschmann and the St. Louis Symphony Orchestra—Victor 118592, one 12".

Glinka, *Overture* to *Ruslan and Ludmilla*—Eugene Ormandy and the Philadelphia Orchestra—Columbia 19010, one 10".

Gluck, *Overture* to *Alceste*—Wilhelm Fürtwangler and the Berlin Philharmonic Orchestra—Capitol-Telefunken 81001, one 12".

Gounod, *Ballet Music* from *Faust*—George Weldon and the City of Birmingham Orchestra—Columbia Set X 304, two 12".

Mascagni, *Intermezzo* from *Cavalleria Rusticana*—Arthur Fiedler and the Boston "Pops" Orchestra—Victor 4303, one 10".

Mozart, *Overture* to *Don Giovanni*—Sir Thomas Beecham and the London Philharmonic Orchestra—Columbia 70365, one 12".

Overture to *The Marriage of Figaro*—Sir Thomas Beecham and the London Philharmonic Orchestra—Columbia 71606, one 12".

Nicolai, *Overture* to *The Merry Wives of Windsor*—Sir Thomas Beecham and the London Philharmonic Orchestra—Columbia 71622, one 12".

Ponchielli, *Dance of the Hours* from *La Gioconda*—Frederick Stock and the Chicago Symphony Orchestra—Columbia 11621, one 10".

Prokofieff, *March, Scene of Prince and Princess,* and *Scene Infernal* from *The Love of Three Oranges*—Leopold Stokowski and the NBC Symphony Orchestra—Victor 18497, one 12".

Rossini, *Overture to The Barber of Seville*—Arturo Toscanini and the Philadelphia Orchestra—Victor 7225, one 12″.

Overture to William Tell—Arthur Fiedler and the Boston "Pops" Orchestra—Victor Set 456, two 10″.

Smetana, *Overture, Polka,* and *Dance of the Comedians* from *The Bartered Bride*—Sir Thomas Beecham and the Royal Philharmonic Orchestra—Victor Set 1294, two 12″.

Strauss, Richard, *Waltzes* from *Der Rosenkavalier*—Bruno Walter and the Berlin Philharmonic Orchestra—Columbia 67892, one 12″.

Dance from *Salome*—Sir Thomas Beecham and the Royal Philharmonic Orchestra—Victor 12-2344, one 12″.

Wagner, *Prelude to Act III* of *Lohengrin*—Arturo Toscanini and the New York Philharmonic Orchestra—Victor Set 308, five 12″.

Overture to *Die Meistersinger*—Arturo Toscanini and the NBC Symphony Orchestra—Victor 11-9385, one 12″.

Prelude and *Liebestod* from *Tristan und Isolde*—Wilhelm Fürtwangler and the Berlin Philharmonic Orchestra—Victor Set 653, two 12″.

Weber, *Overture* to *Oberon*—Sir Thomas Beecham and the London Philharmonic Orchestra—Columbia 69410, one 12″.

Weinberger, *Polka* and *Fugue* from *Schwanda*—Eugene Ormandy and the Philadelphia Orchestra—Columbia 12372, one 12″.

ORCHESTRAL COMPOSITIONS (Miscellaneous)

Beethoven, *Twelve Contradances*—Howard Barlow and the Columbia Broadcasting System's Orchestra—Columbia Set X 184, two 12″.

Enesco, *Roumanian Rhapsody No. 1*—Artur Rodzinsky and the Philadelphia Orchestra—Columbia LP 2057, one 12″.

Gounod, *Funeral March of a Marionette*—Eugene Ormandy and the Minneapolis Symphony Orchestra—Victor 8661, one 12″.

Griffes, *The White Peacock*—Howard Hanson and the Eastman-Rochester Orchestra—Victor Set 608, four 12″.

Handel, *Water Music*—Eugene Ormandy and the Philadelphia Orchestra—Columbia Set X 279, two 12″.

Mendelssohn, *Incidental Music to Midsummer Night's Dream*—Arturo Toscanini and the NBC Symphony Orchestra—Victor Set 1280, four 12″.

Milhaud, *Suite Francaise*—Composer conducting the Philharmonic Orchestra—Columbia Set X 268, two 12″.

Mozart, *German Dances*, K 605, Nos. 1, 2, and 3—Bruno Walter and the Vienna Philharmonic Orchestra—Victor 4564, one 10″.

Pierne, *Entrance of the Little Fauns* and *March of the Little Lead Soldiers*—Walter Hendl and the Carnegie "Pops" Orchestra—Columbia 7591, one 12″.

Ravel, *Boléro*—André Kostelanetz and the Robin Hood Dell Orchestra—Columbia Set X 257, two 12″.

Sibelius, *Valse Triste*—Charles O'Connell and the Victor Symphony Orchestra—Victor 36228, one 12″.

Strauss, Johann, *By the Beautiful Blue Danube*—George Szell and the Vienna Philharmonic Orchestra—Victor Set 805, four 12″.

Vivaldi, *Concerto Grosso in D Minor*, opus 3, No. 11—Serge Koussevitsky and the Boston Symphony Orchestra—Victor Set 886, two 12″.

Waldteufel, *Skaters' Waltz*—Arthur Fiedler and the Boston "Pops" Orchestra—Victor 4396, one 10″.

Williams, *Fantasia on a Theme by Thomas Tallis*—Dimitri Mitropoulos and the Minneapolis Symphony Orchestra—Columbia Set X 300, two 12″.

SYMPHONIES

Beethoven, *Symphony No. 3 in E Flat (Eroica)*, opus 55—Bruno Walter and the Philadelphia Orchestra—Columbia Set 858, six 12″.

Symphony No. 5 in C Minor, opus 67—Arturo Toscanini and the NBC Symphony *Orchestra*—Victor Set 417, four 12″.

Symphony No. 9 in D Minor—Bruno Walter and the New York Philharmonic Orchestra—Columbia Set 900, eight 12″.

Brahms, *Symphony No. 1 in C Minor*, opus 68—Arturo Toscanini and the NBC Symphony Orchestra—Victor Set 875, five 12″.

Dvořák, *Symphony No. 5 in E Minor*, opus 95—Leopold Stokowski and his orchestra—Victor Set 1248, five 12″.

Franck, *Symphony in D Minor*—Sir Thomas Beecham and the London Philharmonic Orchestra—Columbia Set 479, five 12″.

Harris, *Symphony No. 3*—Serge Koussevitsky and the Boston Symphony Orchestra—Victor Set 651, two 12″.

Haydn, *Symphony No. 104 in D (London)*—Edwin Fischer and his chamber orchestra—Victor Set 617, three 12″.

Mendelssohn, *Symphony No. 4 in A (Italian)*—Serge Koussevitsky and the Boston Symphony Orchestra—Victor Set 1259, three 12".

Mozart, *°Symphony No. 41 in C (Jupiter)*, K 551—Bruno Walter and the Philadelphia Orchestra—Columbia Set 1259, four 12".

Prokofieff, *°Classical Symphony*—Serge Koussevitsky and the Boston Symphony Orchestra—Victor Set 1241, two 12".

Schubert, *°Symphony No. 8 in B Minor (Unfinished)*—Bruno Walter and the Philadelphia Orchestra—Columbia Set 699, three 12".

Schumann, *Symphony No. 1 in B Flat (Spring)*—Erich Leinsdorf and the Cleveland Orchestra—Columbia Set 617, four 12".

Shostakovitch, *Symphony No. 5*—Artur Rodzinsky and the Cleveland Orchestra—Columbia Set 520, five 12".

Sibelius, *Symphony No. 2 in D*—Sir Thomas Beecham and the Royal Philharmonic Orchestra—Victor Set 1334, five 12".

Tschaikowski, *°Symphony No. 6 (Pathétique)*—Wilhelm Fürtwangler and the Berlin Philharmonic Orchestra—Victor Set 553, six 12".

SYMPHONIC POEMS

Borodin, *On the Steppes of Central Asia*—Constant Lambert and the Philharmonic Orchestra—Columbia 71956, one 12".

Debussy, *La Mer*—Serge Koussevitsky and the Boston Symphony Orchestra—Victor Set 643, three 12".

Gershwin, *°An American in Paris*—Leonard Bernstein and the RCA Victor Orchestra—Victor Set 1237, two 12".

Hindemith, *Mathis der Maler*—Eugene Ormandy and the Philadelphia Orchestra—Victor Set 854, three 12".

Liszt, *Les Préludes*—Leopold Stokowski and his orchestra—Victor Set 1227, two 12".

Saint-Saens, *°Symphonic Poem No. 3 (Danse Macabre)*—Leopold Stokowski and the Philadelphia Orchestra—Victor 14162, one 12".

Sibelius, *The Swan of Tuonela*—Leopold Stokowski and his orchestra—Victor 12-0585, one 12".

Strauss, Richard, *°Till Eulenspiegel*—Serge Koussevitsky and the Boston Symphony Orchestra—Victor Set 1029, two 12".

Stravinsky, *L'histoire du Soldat*—Leonard Bernstein and members of the Boston Symphony Orchestra—Victor Set 1197, four 12".

OVERTURES

Beethoven, *Egmont Overture,* opus 84—Felix Weingartner and the Vienna Philharmonic Orchestra—Columbia 69195, one 12".

Suppé, *Light Cavalry Overture*—Arthur Fielder and the Boston "Pops" Orchestra—Victor 11-9954, one 12".

Tschaikowski, *Romeo and Juliet Overture*—Arturo Toscanini and the NBC Symphony Orchestra—Victor Set 1178, three 12".

PIANO MUSIC

Bach, *Jesu, Joy of Man's Desiring*—Dame Myra Hess— Victor 4538, one 10".

Fantasy and Fugue in D—Guiomar Novaës—Columbia X 298, two 10".

Beethoven, *Sonata No. 14 in C-sharp Minor,* opus 27, No. 2—Rudolph Serkin—Columbia Set X 237, two 12".

Brahms, *Intermezzi,* opus 76, Nos. 3 and 4, opus 116, No. 4, opus 118, No. 6, and opus 119, No. 2—Walter Geiseking—Columbia Set Z 201, two 12".

Chopin, *Polonaise No. 6 in A Flat,* opus 53—Vladimir Horowitz—Victor 11-9065, one 12".

Scherzo No. 4 in E, opus 54—Vladimir Horowitz—Victor 14634, one 12".

Debussy, *Children's Corner*—Alfred Cortot—Victor 7147–8, two 12".

Liszt, *Hungarian Rhapsody No. 6*—Vladimir Horowitz—Victor Set 1165, three 12".

Mozart, *Sonata in C Minor,* K 457—Walter Geiseking—Columbia Set X 93, two 12".

Scarlatti, *Sonata No. 104 in C*—Dame Myra Hess—Columbia 4083, one 10".

Schumann, *Carnaval*—Dame Myra Hess—Victor Set 476, three 12".

Weber, *Invitation to the Dance*—Benno Moisevitch—Victor 18050, one 12".

SACRED SONGS

Bach, *Now Let Every Tongue Adore Thee*—Dorothy Maynor, soprano—Victor 11-9108, one 12".

Haydn, *In Native Worth* from *The Creation*—Aksel Schitz, tenor—His Master's Voice DB 5271, one 12".

Recordings for Children

A recent phenomenon in the recording industry is the tremendous growth in the sales of a group of recordings labeled "children's recordings." A few years ago this area of recordings was only a moderately lucrative sideline for recording companies. Today, it represents a major source of revenue for some of the larger companies, and several new companies operate exclusively in the area. There is a wide range of quality in the recordings. Some of them are unbelievably cheap and trivial, while others are thoughtfully produced, tasteful, and sound from both a musical and an educational point of view.

One of the unfortunate implications of the label "children's recordings" is that children may listen to no other kind of recordings. There is no doubt that recordings made especially for children are desirable and that they fill a need. On the other hand, it is regrettable if children's listening is limited to recordings so labeled. Children love to listen to all kinds of music within their comprehension. Many of the great composers have written music especially for children, and a great deal of standard music literature is equally suitable for children and adults.

Anyone who is concerned with the recreation of children needs to be familiar with recordings suitable for them. The recordings on this list represent the author's judgment as to desirable recordings for children from the ages of five to eleven. They are selected from both "children's recordings" and standard recordings. The list is organized in three categories: instrumental music, vocal music, and stories with music.

INSTRUMENTAL MUSIC

Air for the G String—Bach—Victor 7103
Andantino—Thomas—Victor 20079
Barcarolle from *Tales of Hoffman*—Offenbach—Victor 11-9174
The Blue Danube Waltz and *Tales of the Vienna Woods*—Strauss—
    Victor 15425
Carnival of the Animals—Saint-Saens—Victor MO 785

Clair de Lune—Debussy—Columbia 72080D
Coppélia Ballet Suite—Delibes—Victor DM 1305
Country Dances—Mozart—Young People's Records 313
Dance of the Hours from *La Gioconda*—Ponchielli—Victor 11833
Danse Macabre—Saint-Saens—Victor 14162
Minuet from *Don Giovanni*—Mozart—Victor 1199
El Capitan and *Washington Post March*—Sousa—Victor 4501
The Elfin Dance—Grieg—Victor 20079
Entrance of the Little Fauns—Pierne—Victor 4319
Evening Bells—Kullak—Victor 20079
Famous American Marches (Goldman Band)—Victor P 5
Fiddle Faddle and *Chicken Reel*—Victor 10-1397
Gavotte from *Mignon*—Thomas—Victor 7456
Grand Canyon Suite—Grofé—Victor DM 1038
Hansel and Gretel (Overture)—Humperdinck—Victor 9075
Hungarian Dances—Brahms—Victor 4321
Invitation to the Dance—Weber—Victor 15189
The Little Brass Band—Young People's Records 703
The Little White Donkey—Ibert—Decca Album 85
March of the Dwarfs—Grieg—Victor 22177
March of the Little Lead Soldiers—Pierne—Victor 4314
March of the Toys—Herbert—Victor 12592
Minuet—Boccherini—Victor 7256
Moment Musical—Schubert—Victor 11-9174
Morning from *Peer Gynt*—Grieg—Columbia MX 180
Mother Goose Suite—Ravel—Columbia MX 320
The Music of Aaron Copland—Young People's Records 408
Narcissus—Nevin—Victor 20443
Nocturne from *Midsummer Night's Dream*—Mendelssohn—Victor 6677
The Nutcracker Suite—Tschaikowski—Victor DM 1020
On Wings of Song—Mendelssohn—Victor 6848
An Organ Concert of Carols—Columbia 6076
Rodeo—Copland—Victor DM 1214
Rondino—Kreisler—Columbia 17408D
Rondo for Bassoon and Orchestra—Weber—Young People's Records 1009
Schön Rosmarin—Kreisler—Victor 1386
Slavonic Dances—Dvořák—Victor 11-8566
The Sleeping Beauty—Tschaikowski—Victor 11932
The Swan—Saint-Saëns—Victor 1143

Three Dances from *The Bartered Bride*—Smetana—Columbia 71049D

To a Wild Rose and *To a Water Lily*—MacDowell—Victor 1152

Toy Symphony—Haydn—Young People's Records 1001

William Tell Overture—Rossini—Victor LM 14

Young Person's Guide to the Orchestra—Britten—Columbia MM703

VOCAL MUSIC

A-Hunting We Will Go—Young People's Records 505

American Folk Songs (Eli Siegmeister)—Victor P-41

Animal Fair (Burl Ives)—Columbia MJV 59

Another Sing Along—Young People's Records 723

Christmas Carols of Many Lands (Vienna Boys' Choir)—Victor C 32

Christmas Hymns (Collegiate Chorale)—Victor 11-8672

Christmas Music by the Boys' Town Choir—Capitol 4914

Danish Songs (Lauritz Melchior)—Columbia M-542

Deep River (Marian Anderson)—Victor 2032

The Don Cossacks on the Attack—Columbia M-542

Folk Songs and Ballads of America (Margeret Dodd)—Hargail HN 705

Grandfather's Farm—Children's Record Guild 5004

Hymns for Children—Columbia MJV 65

The Little Red Wagon—Children's Record Guild—1004

Mary Doodle (Susan Reed)—Children's Record Guild 5014

More Playtime Songs—Young People's Records 729

Mother Goose Songs (Burl Ives)—Columbia MJV 67

Oklahoma Selections—Decca DD 359

On Lemmer Lemmer Street—Children's Record Guild 5006

Ride 'Em, Cowboy—Children's Record Guild 5001

Sea Chanties (Leonard Warren)—Victor MO 1186

The Sing Song Man—Decca CUS 23

Sing Along—Young People's Records 722

Sing, Cowboy, Sing—Capitol AC-77

Songs from the Veld—Decca 471 and A 302

Songs of Stephen Foster (Nelson Eddy)—Columbia MM745 **and** MM795

Spirituals (Marian Anderson)—Victor MO 1238

Spirituals (Dorothy Maynor)—Victor M 879

Swing Low, Sweet Chariot (Paul Robeson)—Columbia MM819

The Wayfaring Stranger (Burl Ives)—Columbia C 103

Welsh Traditional Songs—Victor M 965

STORIES WITH MUSIC

Bambi—Victor Y 391
The Boy Who Sang for the King—Victor Y 376
The Carrot Seed—Children's Record Guild 1003
Chicken Licken and *The Gingerbread Boy*—Decca CUS 8
Chisholm Trail—Young People's Records 409
Cinderella—Victor Y 399
Cinderella—Children's Record Guild 201
The Emperor's New Clothes—Young People's Records 1007-8
The Great Big Parade—Allegro Junior 25
The Hunter's Horn—Young People's Records 421
Iolanthe—Allegro Intermediate 57
Jazz Band—Young People's Records 410
Licorice Stick—Young People's Records 420
The Neighbors' Band—Young People's Records 726
Pancho Goes to a Fiesta—Columbia MJV 48
Pee Wee, the Piccolo—Victor Y 344
Peter and the Wolf—Columbia MM477; Victor M 566 and Y 386
Said the Piano to the Harpsichord—Young People's Records 411
Ship Ahoy—Children's Record Guild 5003
There Were Three Indians—Metro-Goldwyn-Mayer S-4
Train to the Zoo—Children's Record Guild 1001
Tubby, the Tuba—Decca CU 106
'Twas the Night Before Christmas—Columbia MJV 88
Underground Train—Young People's Records 407
A Walk in the Forest—Young People's Records 805
Working on the Railroad—Young People's Records 427

SELECTION AND CARE OF RECORDING EQUIPMENT

The selection of good equipment is an important factor in attaining the utmost in enjoyment from listening to recordings. Inadequate equipment inevitably reduces the satisfaction of listening to music and, conversely, good machinery increases the listener's pleasure.

The Phonograph

The most important and most expensive item of equipment is, of course, the phonograph. Phonographs range in price from a few dollars to over a thousand, the cost depending to a great extent upon the nature of the cabinet which has little or no effect upon the tone or playing qualities of the machine. When available funds are limited, it is wise to sacrifice elegance and beauty in the cabinet and spend the money to secure the best possible working parts.

Several reputable companies make phonographs which are suitable for individual or organization use. Another possibility is to assemble a phonograph by purchasing the component parts separately—an amplifier, a speaker, a cabinet (or baffle), a record changer or turntable, and a pick-up. Consumers' Union (38 East First Street, New York) has a complete set of instructions for assembling a phonograph; it may be secured for fifty cents. Any person with a reasonable amount of mechanical aptitude can do the job.

In purchasing a phonograph, consideration should be given to fidelity of reproduction, speed, simplicity of operation, and needle pressure.

FIDELITY OF REPRODUCTION

The best test of fidelity of reproduction is to have several qualified and experienced listeners hear the phonograph and judge whether it sounds good. Extremely high fidelity is an expensive quality and is unnecessary for most purposes. Many listeners prefer the mellowness of tone that is characteristic of instruments of medium-high fidelity. Furthermore, only an excellent high-fidelity recording sounds better on a high-fidelity phonograph. All that a high-fidelity phonograph gets out of the average recording is more surface noise and a slightly better bass tone.

SPEED

After a period of uncertainty and indecision, the matter of record speed has become quite well stabilized. Most of the recording companies are issuing both standard recordings that operate at 78 revolutions per minute and long-playing microgroove recordings that operate at 33⅓ revolutions per minute. A phonograph should by all means play at both speeds. Almost all recorded music is available on records that operate at one or both of these two speeds, with the exception of some short compositions and popular selections which are on 45-r.p.m. recordings. If a person wishes to play recordings that operate at 45 revolutions per minute, he is advised to purchase a separate phonograph or a separate turntable that plugs into a phonograph. Most of the three-speed phonographs are too complicated and cumbersome for satisfactory general use in a recreation center.

It is essential that the turntable maintains a uniform rate of speed. The effect of variations in speed is apparent at 78 revolutions per minute and is particularly obvious and annoying at the slower speeds.

SIMPLICITY OF OPERATION

All the switches and controls on a phonograph should be simple, in clear view, and properly labeled. Complexity of operation is a drawback in any phonograph and is a particular disadvantage in one that is being used by several people. In addition, complicated machines are likely to get out of adjustment and to require frequent servicing.

NEEDLE PRESSURE

The needle pressure should be about one ounce on standard-speed recordings and about one-fifth of an ounce on long-playing microgroove recordings. Pressure that is significantly greater results in excessive record wear.

The Needles

The choice of a good needle is of great importance in getting the most out of recordings and in prolonging their life. Each playing of a recording results in some wear, and one or two playings with a poor needle can ruin a new recording. On the other hand, with a good needle, a recording can be played hundreds of times without obvious deterioration. Needles are either nonpermanent or semipermanent. "Permanent," as often applied to needles, is a glaring misnomer, except, perhaps, in the case of diamond points. Any needle wears down eventually and must be changed at the first audible sign of wear.

Several kinds of needles are available, including ordinary steel needles and those with points of precious metal, cactus or fiber needles, and needles made from precious stones, such as sapphires and diamonds.

STEEL NEEDLES

The familiar steel needles in envelopes of twenty-five or fifty are unsatisfactory for any use. The points are not accurately machined and have to wear down to fit the grooves in the recording. Since the steel is much harder than the material of the recording, it is obvious that the recording is going to be worn considerably in the process of playing.

There are better grades of steel needles which give satisfactory service. Five or ten of these are usually packaged on a card. Their points are more accurately machined and do not cause excessive wear if a light pick-up is used. They are good for only a few records and must be changed at the first sign of wear.

Steel needles tipped with tungsten or other durable precious metals are also available. These are very satisfactory if the pick-up is light. They last considerably longer than other steel needles, but cannot be considered even semipermanent. They must be changed at the first sign of wear.

FIBER OR CACTUS NEEDLES

Although it is commonly assumed that needles made of cactus or fiber cause the least record wear, this is by no means true. These needles lose their points rapidly and need to be sharpened after one side of a record is played. Home sharpening produces an inferior point, results in a dull tone, and damages the record. Needles of this type are not recommended.

SAPPHIRE AND DIAMOND POINT NEEDLES

Frequent needle changing is a nuisance with any phonograph and with an automatic record changer the desirability of a more permanent needle is obvious. Sapphires and diamonds are the two stones most often used in making needles of a more permanent nature. The sapphire point produces excellent results, but can be considered only semipermanent. On long-playing microgroove recordings, the deterioration of the sapphire point is especially rapid and results in progressive deterioration in recordings after about fifteen hours of use. The sapphire point must be changed at the first audible sign of wear.

The diamond point is in every respect superior to all other types. Although no material can be considered permanent, the diamond, the hardest of the jeweled points, retains its shape and has a life expectancy many times that of other points. The initial cost of the diamond point is considerably higher, but its durability and superior performance make it an excellent investment. Needle wear is greater on microgroove recordings than on standard recordings. For this reason, the diamond point, while preferable for all recordings, is almost indispensable for microgroove recordings.

The Record Cabinet

Proper storage is an important element in the preservation of recordings. The record collector should buy or build an adequate record cabinet. A closed, dustproof cabinet is preferable. The cabinet must be kept away from direct heat which causes recordings to warp. The shelves should be a minimum of fourteen inches high and fifteen inches deep, in order to house albums of all sizes and to allow sufficient room in which the hand may remove and replace albums. Albums should be kept on the shelves in vertical position. Stacking one album on top of another is almost certain to result in broken or warped recordings.

Albums should be stored in their original packages, and single recordings placed in miscellaneous albums of appropriate size.

More than one recording should never be placed in one envelope of an album. The most convenient arrangement for storing recordings on a shelf is by composer, in alphabetical order.

The Card Catalogue

For an extensive collection, a card catalogue, showing all the recordings in the library, proves desirable. It is essential that any organization or institution maintain such a catalogue. Several persons undoubtedly will be using recordings from the library, and a card catalogue serves as a means of locating records quickly. It is also necessary in order to safeguard the collection and keep account of the recordings.

A good card catalogue consists of a three-by-five card for each album or separate recording. Each card shows the name of the composer, the title of the composition including the opus number, the full names of the principal performing artists, the name of the record company, the catalogue number, the price, and the number and size of records. For an extensive library, a cross index—by the name of the artist, the type of composition, and so forth—is desirable.

Care

Recordings represent a long-term investment and deserve the best of care. With careful and intelligent treatment, they will continue to give pleasure for years.

Recordings are properly handled only by the edges. Grasping the surface with the hand results in spots of perspiration and oil from the fingers; these cause surface noise and a dull tone. Before being played a record should be brushed with a record brush or wiped with a soft, clean, slightly damp cloth to remove any dust or grit from the surface. Dust not only wears out records, but also produces surface noise and static, especially on long-playing records.

If the phonograph operates manually, the record should be placed on the turntable before starting it, and allowed to attain full speed before lowering the needle. The needle should be lowered to the ungrooved portion of the disc, adjacent to the starting groove, and slowly guided until it settles into the groove. When using an automatic record changer, one should never interfere with the operation of the changer.

The operator should be alert for any audible sign of needle wear and should change the needle frequently if nonpermanent needles are being used. A needle should never be reused after it has been removed from the pick-up.

After a recording has been played, the tone arm should be raised immediately, and the recording returned to its album, unless it is to be replayed. Stacking loose recordings, or leaving them lying around unprotected, invites breakage, scratches, and other damage.

A cracked recording should never be played. To do so inevitably damages the needle and is liable to harm the pick-up.

CHAPTER FOUR

RECREATION

THROUGH SINGING

Singing is the most natural form of musical participation. Children begin at an early age to sing about all sorts of things—their toys, their dolls, their pets, and the members of the family. Singing is for them a means of personal expression. They love to sing, and do so for the pure joy of it. Most adults continue to sing all through life. They sing alone at different times—in the bath, at work, or while walking or driving an automobile. This solitary activity gives them a lift and an opportunity to express their feelings and emotions.

Music is a social art. Its best setting is one where it is shared with other people. Singing in a group is consistent with and appeals to man's social nature. Everyone enjoys joining in song with other people.

The recreation singing program has traditionally been confined to informal community singing. Although a major emphasis on community singing is proper, a recreation program that operates only in this limited context fails to meet the needs of all the people whom it seeks to serve.

Many people need and desire a broader and more specialized singing experience than community singing provides. Many of them have special interest and unusual ability in singing. If this ability is nurtured and developed, it can be used to enrich the whole recreation program. The purpose of this chapter is to present a general discussion of all the singing activities—community singing, choral singing, and voice classes.

COMMUNITY SINGING

The term "community singing" is used here in a broad sense to refer to the informal singing of any group of people, whether they are drawn from a town, a community, a club or organization, a school, a camp, or a family. This is often the core of the musical activities of such groups. It serves to unify homogeneous organizations, to give the members a common interest and a joint activity, and to promote good fun and fellowship. When a heterogeneous group of people gather together, as so often happens at public meetings, community singing breaks down barriers, helps the people to get acquainted, and creates a harmonious setting for pursuing the purpose for which they assembled.

Community singing has value as an end in itself. All people love to sing and cherish the opportunity to gather together for that express purpose. Singing is a morale builder. In times of social and political unrest, it is a means of constructive emotional release. Singing keeps people cheerful and happy. It provides contact with beauty and opportunity for the expression of almost limitless moods and emotions. Singing refreshes the spirit. It adds zest to living and helps people forget for a while their problems and worries.

People may sing together with or without a song leader. When the group is small and in an intimate situation, spontaneous singing without a leader is more desirable. If the group is large and spread out, a director is necessary to bring the efforts of the group into focus and to secure the best results.

Singing without a Leader

For successful singing without a leader, the group must be small and in a face-to-face situation—for example, seated around a campfire, around a table, or in a small room. Although a leader is not necessary, someone must serve as a lead-off man to get the group started with one or two songs. After the initial songs, he may begin the songs suggested by other members of the group, if those suggesting the songs do not want to lead off. The lead-off man does not direct the singing, but coordinates the efforts of the group. Informality and spontaneity are the outstanding characteristics of this type of singing, and it is important that no one person dominate the group. Everybody should feel free to suggest a song, to start it, to sing any part he desires, and to sing a solo if he wishes.

Singing in parts greatly enhances the pleasure of this type of singing. The singers who have difficulty singing a part should be encouraged to sit next to someone who sings their part. A quartet of good singers which can serve as a nucleus for part singing is an effective means of improving the quality of the singing.

The singing may be done with or without accompaniment. Piano, guitar, ukelele, autoharp, and accordion are excellent accompanying instruments. If none of these is available, a melody-playing instrument, such as a violin or trumpet, may be used. For many songs, an accompaniment by rhythm instruments such as tambourines, castanets, or wooden blocks is effective, either alone or in combination with other instruments. For accompanied singing, it is well to have the accompanist serve as lead-off man. For unaccompanied singing, the person beginning the song may get the pitch by ear or from a pitch pipe. If one person in the group has a good ear, he should sound the beginning pitch for all the songs by singing the first phrase or singing the chord on which the song begins.

The songs for this type of singing should be familiar, simple, and not too rapid in tempo. Songs with a solo for the leader and a chorus for the group are ideal. Other suitable types of songs are spirituals, hymns, sea chanteys, and songs with "barber shop" harmony.

Singing with a Leader

In many situations, singing without a leader is not feasible. If the singers are not seated face to face, if the group is large, or if the songs are difficult, a leader is necessary for satisfactory results. He announces the songs, leads them, and encourages the group to sing.

Singing with a leader has many recreational possibilities. It is appropriate at community meetings planned for the sole purpose of singing, at religious and patriotic services, at school assemblies, at dinners, and at civic club, social, and camp gatherings. In other words, it is appropriate whenever a large group of people are assembled, regardless of the primary purpose of the occasion.

Singing with a leader has much greater musical possibilities than singing without a leader. A skilled leader can make singing a worth-while and thrilling musical experience for all the participants. With a leader, a group can sing a wide variety of music, ranging from the simplest folk songs to exquisite art songs. The leader helps the group interpret the songs in a manner that will give the singers great satisfaction.

The physical situation has a great effect upon singing. The room or area must be arranged so that all the singers can see the song leader, and they must all face in his direction. An elevated position for the leader is desirable. If there is no stage or risers, he may stand on a table. He must be close enough to the group for all to hear his instructions and his singing. For a very large group, a public address system may be necessary.

Although the absence of accompaniment does not preclude this type of singing, a satisfactory accompaniment is essential for the best results. The accompanist should be close to the leader and audible to the entire group. The piano is the best accompanying instrument, but an organ, electric guitar, or accordion may be used. The ukelele, guitar, and autoharp lack sufficient volume for accompanying large groups, but they may be used in combinations. Instrumental ensembles, orchestras, and bands provide excellent accompaniments for the singing of large groups.

For successful singing, the group must have access to the words of the songs. Song books, song slides, or song sheets should be purchased for this purpose. Printing or mimeographing copyrighted words is an infringement of copyright laws and is punishable by a fine.

Song books are generally most satisfactory because they have both words and music. For best results, there should be one book for each two singers. Several excellent, inexpensive song books are listed on pages 78 to 80.

Commercial song sheets are inexpensive and satisfactory for many occasions, although they lack musical notation and are fragile and easily rumpled or lost. Sources of song sheets are cited on page 80.

If song books or song sheets are used, provision should be made for orderly distribution before the singing and for collection after the singing is over. For groups which sing together regularly, it is preferable to make each person responsible for his own song book or song sheets.

Commercial song slides are also inexpensive, but they require a projector, a screen, and darkness. When thrown on the screen, slides insure that the singers look in the direction of the song leader, but a darkened room often has an unfortunate effect on the singing.

SONGS FOR COMMUNITY SINGING

The success of community singing depends more upon the songs used than upon any other single factor. Songs for community singing need not all be trivial and banal. It is a fallacious idea that amateur singers have to limit themselves to songs on the level of *Goodnight Ladies.* It is true that songs of this type have a definite place in the community singing, and give great pleasure, but the pleasure of singing is greatly increased if a wider range of music literature is used. There is a place in community singing for all types of songs, from humorous jingles to the finest art song. Action songs, art songs, folk songs, hymns, popular songs, rounds, spirituals, and work songs are all appropriate for community singing. Descriptions of all these types of songs follow:

Action Songs

Action songs are songs in which the words call for actions to the rhythm. They are usually of a humorous nature. They are excellent for "ice-breakers" and for bringing boisterous and good-natured fun into the singing. Many people who are hesitant about singing will join the actions and forget themselves sufficiently to begin singing. Children and young people are especially fond of action songs. Adults are occasionally resistant to participation in action songs, but a skillful leader can put them over with any group.

Art Songs

Art songs are poetry set to music for solo voice. Most of the great composers have written in this medium (see pages 27 to 28), and these songs provide a wonderful opportunity for intimate contact with some of the finest music of the world. Although art songs are not specifically written for singing by groups, many of them are suitable for this purpose and offer a stirring musical and esthetic experience. It is desirable for groups to sing them in unison with the original accompaniment. Art songs require more musical insight and skill on the part of the song leader than other types of songs, but there need be no hesitation about using them, if the voice range is not excessive and the melodies are not too elaborate for the group to handle.

Folk Songs

Folk songs are songs that have grown out of the life, culture, and hearts of various peoples of the world. They were originally improvised by individuals or groups, and have been handed down through hearing from person to person and from generation to generation. Often several slightly different versions of folk songs exist. These songs are an excellent means of developing an appreciation of one's own culture and an understanding of other cultures of the world. They are ideal for group singing, because of their simplicity and their closeness to the life of the people.

Hymns

Hymns are religious songs of praise, designed for performance by the entire congregation in religious services. Hymns constitute an enduring segment of music literature and an important part of the cultural heritage. They are profoundly expressive and have almost universal appeal. Among the loveliest hymns are the chorales, the hymn tunes of the German Protestant church. Although many composers have harmonized chorales, those written by Johann Sebastian Bach are the finest and best known. Most hymns have a limited vocal range, avoid complex rhythms and melodic skips, and have simple but rich harmonies. These qualities make them ideal for group singing.

Popular Songs

Popular songs are usually light in character and often are written for social dancing. They strike the fancy of the public for a short time; then most of them are soon forgotten. A few, however, are quite suitable for community singing. They have great appeal for adolescents and offer an excellent point of departure for their singing. Any current or old popular song may be used, if the melody is attractive and the words are not objectionable. Songs from musical shows are often very suitable. Jazz songs and other songs written especially for dancing are seldom good for group singing.

Rounds

Rounds are songs with a single melody line so constructed that a harmonious result is attained when each of two or more groups begin to sing the melody at a stated interval. Each group sings through the song the same number of times, usually three. Rounds are an excellent means of introducing part singing.

Spirituals

Spirituals are songs that have grown directly out of the religious life of the Negro race. They cut across all lines of religious belief and are treasured and loved by members of every creed. They constitute an outstanding cultural contribution of the Negro race and serve well to promote racial understanding and appreciation. Spirituals are among the loveliest and most poignant of songs and are notable for their rich, full harmony. The words are usually repetitious and easy to remember. Conceived for singing by groups, they offer a truly satisfying esthetic experience for amateur singers.

Work Songs

Work songs are songs that have grown out of occupations that have engaged men through the years. Originally, the workers improvised these songs and sang them as an accompaniment to their tasks. One of the original purposes of work songs was to achieve rhythm and coordination for such tasks as raising a sail or rowing a boat. As a result, they are highly rhythmic, and the words and melodies are usually simple. The words are repetitious and are often arranged in sections to be sung alternately by the leader and the group. Work songs have strong appeal for adolescents, particularly boys. Outstanding among work songs are sea chanteys, railroad songs, and boat songs.

CHORAL SINGING

Choral singing refers to the singing of groups which are organized for the sole purpose of singing and which rehearse regularly with a director. Choral singing is a traditional form of recreation for many nationalities. Choral societies are an important part of the social and cultural tradition of the German and British people, and many American communities have carried on the tradition.

Choral singing is a more specialized activity than community singing. The songs are generally more difficult and of higher caliber. Choral singing requires intensive rehearsal on a limited number of songs. It is more highly organized, with each singer assigned to sing a specific part. The emphasis in choral singing is on polished, musicianly performance, with the ultimate goal of performing in public.

There are several different types of choral organizations: mixed chorus, men's glee club, women's glee club, and small singing ensembles. Each type of organization has a place in the recreational singing program.

The Mixed Chorus

The mixed chorus is the most desirable of the choral organizations from both recreational and musical points of view. Since it is composed of both men and women, it provides a natural social situation. The blending of male and female voices, with their wide range in pitch and quality, has tremendous possibilities for expressiveness and beauty. Another argument strongly in favor of the mixed chorus is that the finest choral music of the world is written for mixed voices and that there is an almost endless supply of material of varying difficulty. The mixed chorus brings a highly satisfying musical experience both to the singers and to the people who listen to the singing. Mixed choruses may range in size from twenty to several hundred singers.

The voice parts in the mixed chorus are usually soprano, alto, tenor, and bass. If the group is inexperienced or immature, two-part (soprano and bass) or three-part (soprano, alto, and bass) arrangements may be used initially, but the introduction of four-part choruses should be delayed no longer than necessary.

The Men's Glee Club

The men's glee club is a popular and attractive form of choral singing which also has a strong appeal for both singers and listeners. Singing in close harmony by a group of men has a robust and colorful quality that is fascinating and thrilling. The music for men's glee club is generally somewhat inferior in quality to that for mixed chorus. The great composers have seldom written music in this medium, but many arrangements of all kinds of music are available.

The voice parts in the men's glee club are first tenor, second tenor, baritone, and bass. There are arrangements in two or three parts, but the reduction in the number of parts definitely reduces the effectiveness of the singing.

The Women's Glee Club

Although a women's glee club lacks the variety of the mixed chorus and the virility of the men's chorus, it has a charm and beauty all its own. The singing of a good women's chorus has a lyrical, ethereal quality that has attracted several of the great operatic and oratorio composers. There is a wealth of material for this kind of group.

The voice parts of the women's glee club are usually first soprano, second soprano, and alto. Other common arrangements are in two parts (soprano and alto) and in four parts (first soprano, second soprano, first alto, and second alto).

Other Singing Groups

In addition to the large choral organizations, there are several types of small singing groups. The most popular is the men's quartet. Although the men's quartet is usually associated with "barbershop" singing, its repertory can and should include a wide variety of suitable music. Another excellent small group is a trio of women singing popular songs in close harmony, a style popularized by the Andrews sisters and other professional groups. Other vocal combinations are the mixed quartet and the women's quartet.

Requisites for the Choral Program

The first requisite for a good choral program is a competent choral director. Directing choral organizations requires specialized knowledge, ability, and experience. The choral director should have an acceptable singing voice, should understand the technique of vocal production, should have a good conducting technique, should have facility in reading music, and, last but not least, should be able to get along with people and make them want to sing. The average recreation worker is not qualified to direct choral organizations and should not attempt to do so. From the public schools or one of the churches, every community can secure the part-time services of a qualified choral director.

An adequate rehearsal room is essential. The rehearsal room needs good lighting and a sufficient number of chairs to seat the group. The chairs are best arranged in a semicircle around the director and, preferably, on risers. A well-tuned piano and a music stand for the director complete the necessary room equipment.

An expanding library of suitable music is necessary. It is wise to keep the music in the library and to distribute it for each rehearsal. At the end of each rehearsal the music should be collected and accounted for. A list of recommended books for choral singing appears on pages 80 to 83.

A good choral program requires regular rehearsals and good attendance. Very little can be accomplished without regular rehearsals with all the singers present. One two-hour rehearsal each week is satisfactory in most situations. In setting the day and time for the rehearsal, consideration should be given to the preferences of the singers.

Public performances give impetus to the choral program. Choral rehearsals without the prospect of public appearance lose their spirit. Looking forward to appearing in public spurs on the singers and gives purpose to their rehearsals. On the other hand, too frequent public appearances become a burden on both singers and director. If the frequency of public appearances makes them a chore instead of a pleasure, the choral program will fail.

VOICE CLASSES

The purpose of voice classes is to teach people how to sing. Vocal instruction has traditionally been carried on in private lessons, but recently voice teachers have developed techniques for teaching the fundamentals of vocal production in classes. Voice classes are an efficient and inexpensive means of giving elementary vocal instruction to large numbers of people and of expanding the vocal repertory.

Although the voice class is a more highly specialized activity than community singing and choral singing, it has a definite place in a well-rounded recreation program. In every group of young people there are those with unusual talent which merits development, and many older people who have never had an opportunity to take voice lessons desire to do so. The voice class meets the needs of both.

The emphasis in voice classes is on the development of individual voices, and the aim of voice classes is to produce singers who can sing alone. Choral singing often results in a feeling of dependence, as far as singing is concerned. Many people who love to sing in a chorus refuse to sing when not with a group. The voice class tends to counteract this feeling of dependence.

The teacher of the voice class must be selected with care. He must be an experienced singer who has a clear understanding of the basic principles of vocal production, breath control, and style in singing. He must be sympathetic with and interested in the purpose of the voice class, and must know and be able to use the methods and techniques of instruction that produce the best results in voice classes.

The size of the voice class may range from ten to twenty persons. A class smaller than ten almost ceases to be a class and becomes a series of short private lessons. It is also an uneconomical use of the instructor's time. A class larger than twenty is cumbersome and leaves no time for the individual attention necessary in this type of work.

The best basis for the organization of voice classes is according to the ranges of the voices. The high voices, both male and female, are grouped together in one class, and the lower voices in another. This arrangement reduces the amount of time spent inactively by members of the class, because the singing is always within the range of all. Another advantage is that everyone can use the same books in the same key. The classes may also be organized on the basis of sex, with the women in one class and the men in another, but most people find the mixed class more enjoyable. For recreation purposes, the mixed class is certainly preferable.

Voice classes should meet twice each week for one hour or, if this is not possible, once each week for two hours. Members of voice classes are normally expected to practice their singing between class meetings. The amount of practice will vary considerably from person to person, and a great deal of outside practice cannot be expected of people who are participating in voice classes for recreation purposes.

Members of the voice classes can be used to advantage as soloists for community and choral singing. Voice classes can enrich and expand the recreational singing program by discovering talented people and developing them into leaders for other phases of the singing program.

MATERIALS FOR THE
SINGING PROGRAM

High-quality materials represent an important factor in the success of the recreational singing program. Happily, there exists a large body of excellent, inexpensive, published materials for all phases of the singing program. Lists of song books and song sheets for community singing, choral collections for choral singing, and instruction books for voice classes follow:

Song Books for Community Singing

All the song books listed below are designed for general use. Most of them are available in paper-bound editions and are relatively inexpensive. Organizations engaging in community singing should select one or more song books for regular use, and purchase the number of copies required for its membership. In addition, it is desirable to purchase at least one copy of each of the other books listed as a source of additional songs.

The Golden Book of Favorite Songs. Hall and McCreary Co.,° 434 S. Wabash Ave., Chicago.

An all-purpose songbook containing 200 of the most widely used community songs.

The "Everybody Sing" Book. Paull-Pioneer Music Corp., 1657 Broadway, New York.

An excellent collection containing a wealth of material of all types. An unique feature is an interchangeable section for mixed or male voices.

The Gray Book of Favorite Songs. Hall and McCreary Co.

A standard collection of community songs and choruses.

The Home and Community Song Book. E. C. Schirmer Music Company, 221 Columbus Ave., Boston.

A superior collection of hymns, chorales, carols, choruses, and folk songs. Contains no stunt songs or novelties. Cloth cover.

Keep On Singing. Paull-Pioneer Music Corp.

An excellent collection containing folk songs, art songs, and other material.

Let Voices Ring. Hall and McCreary Co.

Contains 109 songs, some old favorites and many which are rarely found in community song books.

The New American Song Book. Hall and McCreary Co.

A fine collection of American folk songs and folk songs from other lands. Contains considerable historical information on American folk music. The Pan-American edition includes a group of songs from South America.

The New Blue Book of Favorite Songs. Hall and McCreary Co.

A large collection containing all the songs in *The Golden Book* and *The Gray Book* plus a considerable amount of additional material. Cloth cover.

Ready, Sing! Emerson Books, Inc., 251 W. 19th St., New York.

An excellent small collection of familiar American songs that have stood the test of time. Most of the songs are intended for unison singing. Easy piano accompaniments.

Sing!, C. C. Birchard and Co., 285 Columbus Ave., Boston.

An all-purpose song book containing a wide variety of material.

Sing Again with Harry Wilson. J. J. Robbins and Sons, Inc., 221 W. 47th St., New York.

° Complete address of each publisher is given the first time the publisher is mentioned here.

A new and unusual collection which emphasizes American songs. Contains songs of all types, including popular songs.

Sing Along with Harry Wilson. J. J. Robbins and Sons, Inc.
One of the newer collections. 149 excellent songs of all types from many sources.

Sing and Be Happy. Mills Music, Inc., 1619 Broadway, New York.
Contains a wide variety of community songs, including a number of popular songs. Most of the arrangements are in four parts.

Sing Me Your Songs. Janet E. Tobitt, 416 W. 33rd St., New York.
A good collection of folk songs, art songs, and rounds.

Sing, Men, Sing. (H. and M. Auditorium Series No. 48) Hall and McCreary Co.
An excellent collection of old favorites arranged for three-part male voices.

Sing Together. Girl Scouts, 155 E. 44th St., New York.
A fine collection of songs especially designed for girls' camps.

Singing America. C. C. Birchard and Co.
An excellent collection of 120 songs and choruses. Features folk songs of the Western hemisphere, but a great variety of other material is included.

Sociability Songs. The Rodeheaver Co., 28 E. Jackson Blvd., Chicago.
An inexpensive collection of familiar favorites, including a large number of sacred songs and spirituals.

Songs for Every Purpose and Occasion. Hall and McCreary Co.
An excellent collection containing 350 of the finest community songs. Strong cloth binding.

Songs for Informal Singing. National Recreation Association, 315 Fourth Ave., New York.
A small, inexpensive collection of good songs, containing only melodies and words.

Songs We Sing. Hall and McCreary Co.
An excellent collection containing a wide variety of material and many novelties in texts and arrangements. Complete piano accompaniments are included.

Time to Sing. Edward B. Marks Music Corp., RCA Building, New York.
A varied collection of community songs which includes a large number of the older popular hit songs.

Twice 55 Series. C. C. Birchard and Co.
A comprehensive series of community songbooks that has proved its worth through the years, containing the following volumes:

The New Brown Book—for mixed voices
The New Green Book—for mixed voices
The Blue Book—for male voices
The Rose Book—for treble voices
The Orange Book—for boys' voices
The Red Book—games with music

Universal Folk Songster. G. Schirmer, Inc., 3 East 43rd St., New York.
An excellent collection of folk songs. Most of the arrangements are
for unison singing.

Song Sheets for Community Singing

The National Recreation Association publishes a series of song
sheets which include:

Christmas Carols—words of ten carols
Community Song Booklet—words of 56 old favorites
Easter Carols—words of 10 hymns
Let's Sing the Same Songs—words and melodies of 20 songs
Seven Hymns for Everyone—words only
Songs for Informal Singing—words and melodies of folk songs and
rounds

Other song sheets follow:

Camp Songs. The National Bureau for the Advancement of Music,
315 Fourth Avenue, New York.
Forty-three songs. Keys and sources of music given.
All Join In. Paull-Pioneer Music Corp.
Seventy-five popular community songs. Keys and meters given.
Sing and Be Happy. Mills Music, Inc.
Seventy songs, each with one line of the melody.

Choral Collections for Choral Singing

Choral collections provide music for the choral program with less
expense than octavo editions. Organizations sponsoring a choral
program should purchase several choral collections suitable for
their choral groups. The following list contains choral collections
for mixed voices, girls' and women's voices, and male voices.

MIXED VOICES

These collections encompass a wide range of difficulty. They include arrangements for three parts (soprano, alto, and baritone) and for four parts (soprano, alto, tenor, and bass).

A Choral Digest for S.A.B. Wilson. Paull-Pioneer Music Corp.
> Twenty-three varied choruses arranged for soprano, alto, and baritone. Contains suggestions on vocal production.

Choral Program Series, Book IV. Silver Burdett Co., 45 E. 17th St., New York.
> Easy numbers arranged for soprano, alto, and baritone.

Choral Program Series, Book VI. Silver Burdett Co.
> Moderately difficult numbers for four-part mixed voices.

The Hall and McCreary Auditorium Series. Hall and McCreary Co.
> *Select* A Cappella *Choruses,* No. 1
> Fourteen selections arranged for unaccompanied singing.
> *Select Chorales,* No. 8
> Thirteen chorales arranged for mixed voices in four parts.
> *Spirited Choruses S.A.B.,* No. 18
> Tuneful arrangements in three parts within easy range of boys and girls.

Master Choruses. Smallman and Mathews. Oliver Ditson Co., Bryn Mawr, Pa.
> Forty-nine anthems and choruses of master composers.

Music of Many Lands and Peoples. McConathy, Beattie, and Morgan. Silver Burdett Co.
> A complete and excellent collection of easy choral numbers.

Program Choruses (The Green Book). Hall and McCreary Co.
> A large collection containing numbers of all degrees of difficulty, ranging from unison songs to eight-part *a cappella* choruses.

The Red Book of Program Songs and Choruses. Hall and McCreary Co.
> An excellent, inexpensive collection containing a wealth of material. Most of the songs are arranged for four-part mixed voices. There are several part songs for girls' voices, several for boys' voices, and a few unison songs.

Rounds and Canons. Wilson. Hall and McCreary Co.
> A collection completely devoted to rounds and canons, ranging from easy familiar rounds to difficult concert rounds. Contains instructions for singing rounds.

Senior Laurel Songs. Armitage. C C. Birchard and Co.
> A good standard collection of songs and choruses.

GIRLS' AND WOMEN'S VOICES

These collections contain songs selected and arranged especially for treble voices. Arrangements are in two parts (soprano and alto), three parts (first soprano, second soprano, and alto), and four parts (first soprano, second soprano, first alto, and second alto).

A *Choral Digest for Treble Voices*. Paull-Pioneer Music Corp.
> Twenty-four program numbers with considerable variety. Arrangements are for two-, three-, and four-part treble voices.

Choral Program Series, Book I. Silver Burdett Co.
> Easy two-part numbers for soprano and alto. Several numbers contain optional parts and descants.

Choral Program Series, Book II. Silver Burdett Co.
> Easy to moderately difficult numbers for three parts (soprano, second soprano, and alto) and a few easy four-part numbers.

Concert Songs. Armitage. C. C. Birchard and Co.
> One hundred six numbers arranged for unison, two-, three-, and four-part singing.

The Glenn Glee Club. Glenn and French. Oliver Ditson Co.
> Forty-three folk songs, art songs, and sacred songs arranged for three parts.

The Hall and McCreary Auditorium Series. Hall and McCreary Co.
> *Chorales for Unchanged Voices*, No. 12
> Thirty-odd chorales appropriate for junior choirs.
> *Hymns and Anthems for Treble Choirs*, No. 17
> Fourteen sacred numbers arranged for three parts.

Repertoire: Songs for Women's Voices. Bridgman. American Book Company, 88 Lexington Ave., New York.
> Two volumes of choruses arranged for treble voices.

Song Time For Women's Voices. Paull-Pioneer Music Corp.
> Two- and three-part songs with piano accompaniments.

Three-Part Choruses for Treble Voices. Wilson. Hall and McCreary Co.
> An excellent collection with unusual arrangements and original numbers in modern style.

MALE VOICES

These collections contain choruses that appeal to men and boys. Most of the arrangements for men's voices are in four parts (first tenor, second tenor, baritone, and bass). A few collections are arranged in two and three parts for use by adolescent boys.

Basic Songs for Male Voices. Bridgman. American Book Co.
  A fine, comprehensive collection containing 230 numbers.
Choral Collection. Harold Flammer, 251 W. 19th St., New York.
  Appealing numbers for boys' voices in three parts.
Choral Program Series, Book III. Silver Burdett Co.
  Contains two-, three- and four-part numbers.
Eighteen Easy Choruses. Boston Music Co., 116 Boylston St., Boston.
  Good three-part arrangements.
The Hall and McCreary Auditorium Series. Hall and McCreary Co.
  Famous Spirituals, No. 2
  Forty well-arranged spirituals.
  Singable Songs For Male Voices, No. 9
  Twenty-four songs that men and boys enjoy singing.
  Choruses for Changing Voices, No. 10
  Nineteen selections especially arranged for adolescent boys.
  Part Songs for Changing Voices, No. 11
  Seventeen selections which will interest young people.
  Select Choruses for Boys, No. 21
  Three- and four-part songs within comfortable range of changed and unchanged boys' voices.
  Singable Male Choruses, No. 22
  Easy sacred and secular songs with limited ranges.
Three-Part Choruses for Male Voices. Wilson. Hall and McCreary Co.
  Effective arrangements with limited ranges in the tenor parts.
Twice 55 Part Songs for Boys (The Orange Book). C. C. Birchard and Co., Boston.
  A good collection of songs for adolescent boys' voices. Ranges are limited and there is a wide variety of material.

Instruction Books for Voice Classes

Voice classes require instruction books especially written for a class situation. For this reason, voice methods written for private lessons are seldom suitable for class use. A list of recommended instruction books follows:

CLIPPINGER, D. A. *The Clippinger Class Method of Voice.* Bryn Mawr: Oliver Ditson Co.

HAYWOOD, FREDERICK H. *Universal Song.* New York: G. Schirmer, Inc.

MOONIE, J. A. *Precept and Practice for Singing Class Students.* New York: H. W. Gray Co.

PIERCE, ANNE, AND LIEBLING, ESTELLE. *Class Lessons in Singing.* New York: Silver Burdett Co.

PITTS, CAROL M. *Pitts Voice Class Method.* Chicago: Neil A. Kjos.

TAYLOR, BERNARD. *Group Voice.* New York: G. Schirmer, Inc.

WARD, ARTHUR E. *The Singing Road.* New York: Carl Fischer, Inc.

WILSON, HARRY R. *The Solo Singer.* New York: Carl Fischer, Inc.

CHAPTER FIVE

THE RECREATION
LEADER AND THE
SINGING PROGRAM

Every recreation program should include singing. The recreation leader must understand and appreciate the recreational value of singing and make sure that his program utilizes singing to the fullest possible extent. He should also prepare himself to participate actively in the singing program by learning to lead songs. Whether singing receives major emphasis or is a subsidiary activity, the ability of the recreation leader to sing and lead songs greatly increases his contribution to the program.

THE FUNCTIONS OF THE
RECREATION LEADER

In developing the singing program, the recreation leader should consider the desires and interests of the participants. He should build the program around these desires and interests in such a way that it serves all levels of ability. Suggested functions of the recreation leader in developing the singing program follow:

1. *Organizing community singing as an important recreation activity in itself.* Community singing can stand on its own feet as recreation. It should not be considered just an appendage to other recreation activities. The recreation leader should organize sings on a regular schedule and plan each program around some appropriate central theme.

2. *Encouraging community singing on every appropriate occasion.* People enjoy singing every time they assemble, regardless of the purpose of the meeting. Singing enlivens meetings of all kinds, dinners, hikes, games, parties, and dances. Singing gets

any group of people off to a good start and provides a welcome and refreshing break in the course of a day devoted to work, study, or play.

3. *Extending the music program to care for the needs of all the people he serves.* Although community singing is properly the core of the singing program, it alone cannot fill the needs of everyone. In every group of people there are some who desire a more specialized singing activity. The recreation leader should organize choral groups and voice classes for those who desire them.

4. *Securing the services of qualified music specialists to conduct the choral groups and to teach the voice classes.* Conducting choral groups and teaching voice classes require specialized musical ability and thorough professional preparation. The recreation leader should discover the people in the community who are qualified for this type of work, and secure their services on a part-time basis.

5. *Equipping rehearsal rooms and making other necessary facilities available for the singing program.* The singing program requires rooms which are suitable for community singing, choral rehearsals, and voice classes. If an auditorium is part of the recreational facilities, it may be used for community singing, but it is desirable to have also a specially equipped room for choral rehearsals, a small room for voice classes and small singing ensembles, and, if possible, practice rooms for individuals.

6. *Maintaining a good library of choral music, song books, song sheets, and song slides.* A good singing program requires good material. The recreation leader should seek expert advice in selecting material. For community singing, he should select one or more song-book titles and secure a sufficient number of copies for regular use. In addition, he should buy at least one copy of all the better song books. Song sheets and song slides are desirable to supplement the song books. A list of recommended materials for community singing appears on pages 77 to 80. For the choral program, he should select two or three choral collections, secure enough copies so that each singer has one, and supplement the choral col-

lections with octavo music. A list of recommended choral collections appears on pages 80 to 83. Members of the voice classes normally can be expected to purchase their own material.

The recreation leader should utilize the assistance of volunteer workers in operation of the library, but careful supervision is essential on his part to insure that no music is lost or unduly damaged.

7. *Making arrangements for public performances by the choral groups.* Public performance furnishes a big incentive for choral organizations. The recreation leader should arrange a schedule of performances by the different choral groups, in connection with the recreation program, including both short appearances, as part of other kinds of programs, and one or more concerts each year devoted entirely to choral music. Choral concerts at Christmas and during Music Week are especially appropriate. In addition to performances in connection with the recreation program itself, performances at schools, civic clubs, celebrations, and other public meetings not only give satisfaction to the singers, but also are an excellent means of publicizing the accomplishments of the recreation program.

8. *Organizing festivals and competitions in which the different choral organizations participate.* A choral program thrives on friendly competition. The recreation leader may limit participation in the festival to the choral groups in his own program, or he may invite the participation of groups from other parts of the city or from out-of-town. He should invite an impartial choral specialist to serve as adjudicator and to offer constructive criticism on the performance of each group. A massed chorus composed of all the singers participating in the festival is a thrilling and inspiring finale for a festival.

9. *Exploring, developing, and preserving the folk contribution of the community.* Every section of the country has worthwhile folk music as part of its cultural heritage. The use of this music gives vitality and increased meaning to the recreation singing program. The recreation leader should seek out the folk music

indigenous to the area, preserve it in writing or on recordings, and make it an integral part of the singing program.

10. *Singing, leading songs, and otherwise participating actively in the singing program.* The active participation of the recreation leader in the singing program strengthens the program. If he has to turn the operation of the program over to someone else, the program is under a decided handicap. He should learn to lead songs so that he can incorporate singing with all other phases of the recreation program. His active participation encourages the participation of others.

11. *Discovering individuals with unusual talent and developing leadership for the singing program.* In every group of people there are those with musical talent. If their talent is developed, these people can be a decided asset to the recreation leader and to the singing program. The recreation leader should be able to recognize hidden talent and know how to develop it.

In order to accomplish the last two functions, the recreation leader needs to know as much as possible about community singing and to develop his own ability as a song leader. The remainder of this chapter is devoted to information about song leading that every recreation leader should know.

RECOMMENDED TECHNIQUE OF CONDUCTING AND INTERPRETING SONGS

The job of the song leader is to stimulate group singing and to encourage people to entertain themselves through singing. The qualifications for a song leader are essentially the same as those generally required for leadership in recreation, with the addition of certain musical competencies. The attributes of a good song leader are enthusiasm, sincerity, poise, a sense of humor, a pleasant speaking and singing voice, and musicianship.

The most important qualifications for the song leader are a love of singing and a desire to lead people in singing together for the pure joy of it. A successful song leader must have a friendly, cheerful, outgoing personality. He must be enthusiastic about people and about singing and must be able to spread his enthusiasm among the group.

A song leader needs a strong, clear voice and a good sense of pitch. He needs to have a fundamental knowledge of conducting technique and of the interpretation of music. He needs to be familiar with notation and with the meaning of expression marks. He needs to know how to plan a program of singing, how to present unfamiliar songs, and what kind of accompaniments to use. He must be acquainted with a large number of songs and have a memorized repertory of songs for immediate use. He needs to know how to lead rounds and action songs, how to use descant groups, how to combine songs, and how to promote singing in parts. If he wants to become an expert song leader, he needs to know as much about music as possible and should miss no opportunity to improve his musicianship. He can learn a great deal by observing experienced song leaders, but, needless to say, he will learn the most from actually leading songs.

Conducting Technique

The purpose of conducting is to convey the musical meaning of the songs and the musical ideas of the song leader to the people who are singing. Effective conducting technique entails good posture, knowing how to conduct beats for the meters most common in music, the ability to obtain concerted attacks and releases from the singers, and the ability to communicate ideas on interpretation. In giving directions for posture and conducting beats, it is assumed that the song leader is right-handed. If he is left-handed, he must reverse the directions for the hands and feet.

POSTURE

Posture is an important factor in the appearance of the song leader. A natural posture should be assumed. The leader should not appear stiff and formal. He should stand erect with the right foot slightly in front of the left. The arms should be raised and extended but kept well toward the center of the body. Spreading the feet wide apart and raising the arms high over the head should be avoided. The posture of other song leaders should be observed, and their good postural traits adopted. Practice before a full-length mirror helps to develop an effective posture that exhibits confidence and poise.

BEATS

The most common meters in songs used for community singing are 2/4, 3/4, 4/4, and 6/8. The rhythm of songs in these meters swings in two, three, four, or six beats to the measure. Odd meters with five or seven beats to the measure need not concern the leader of community singing. The right hand is used to mark the rhythm. *Two Beats to the Measure.* If the time signature of a song is 2/4, the rhythm swings in two beats to the measure. A *down-up* motion is used for conducting songs in 2/4 meter. (Diagram 2) *Yankee Doodle* and *Dixie* are popular examples of songs in 2/4 meter.

DIAGRAM 2
Two-Beat Measure.

The same conducting beat is used for songs in 6/8 meter which move at a fast tempo, such as *Solomon Levi* and *When Johnny Comes Marching Home.*
Three Beats to the Measure. If the time signature is 3/4 or 3/8, the rhythm swings in three beats to the measure. A *down-out-up* motion is used for conducting. (Diagram 3) *America* and *The*

Star Spangled Banner are in 3/4 meter. *We Three Kings of Orient Are* is in 3/8 meter.

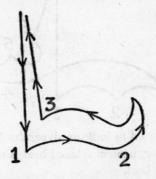

DIAGRAM 3
Three-Beat Measure.

Four Beats to the Measure. If the time signature is 4/4, the rhythm swings in four beats to the measure. A *down-over-out-up* motion is used for conducting. (Diagram 4) *America the Beautiful, Battle Hymn of the Republic,* and *Old Black Joe* are in 4/4 meter.

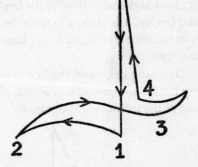

DIAGRAM 4
Four-Beat Measure.

Six Beats to the Measure. If the time signature is 6/8 and the tempo is slow, the rhythm swings in six beats to the measure. A *down-over-over-out-up-up* motion is used for conducting. (Diagram 5)

The Size of the Beat. The size of the beat depends upon the tempo of the song. A fast tempo requires small snappy movements; a slow tempo requires a large free-flowing movement. The beat can also

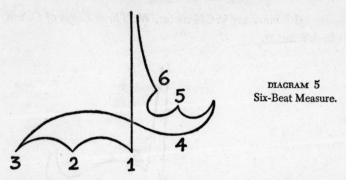

DIAGRAM 5
Six-Beat Measure.

be varied to indicate dynamics (softness and loudness). For soft singing, a small relaxed beat is used; for loud singing, a large intense beat.

ATTACKS

The most critical moment for the song leader is the beginning attack. In order to have all the singers begin together and in the same tempo, a preparatory beat is necessary. Although the preparatory beat varies according to the beat of the measure on which the song begins, it is always in such direction and position that, after its completion, the hand is in place to continue the beat without interruption.

If a song begins on the first beat of the measure, the preparatory beat is an upward movement, similar to that used for the last beat of the measure. (Diagram 6)

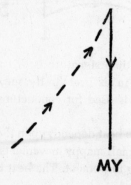

DIAGRAM 6
Preparatory Beat for a Song Beginning on the First Beat of the Measure (*America*).

MY

If the song begins on any but the first beat of the measure, the preparatory beat is an outward motion, followed by a movement that will put the hand in a position to continue the proper pattern for the rhythm. Diagram 7 illustrates the preparatory beat for a song beginning on the last beat of the measure.

DIAGRAM 7
Preparatory Beat for a Song Beginning on the Last Beat of the Measure (*Home on the Range*).

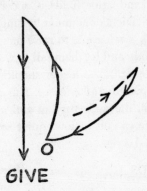

GIVE

If the song begins with a pick-up note that is less than a full beat, the preparatory beat is a downward movement just before the pick-up. (Diagram 8)

DIAGRAM 8
Preparatory Beat for a Song Beginning with a Pick-Up That Is Less Than a Full Beat (*Battle Hymn of the Republic*).

MINE

EYES

To show that he is ready to lead a group in a song, the leader raises both hands to shoulder height and holds them there until the group is alert and ready to sing. Using his right hand, he gives the preparatory beat for the group to begin singing together. He continues to mark the rhythm by moving his right hand in a pattern appropriate to the rhythm of the song.

RELEASES

Releases occur at the end of a song, at phrase endings within a song, and after holds. Concerted releases greatly increase the effectiveness of community singing. The simplest and clearest signal for a release is to raise one or both hands directly in front of the body and let them fall to waist height, bringing them together as they fall. The leader should form the habit of using the same movement for all releases. The movement for the release should be kept in the same rhythm and mood as the song—a smooth, slow release to end a slow, quiet song, a crisp release to end a fast, spirited song.

HOLDS

A hold, or *fermata*, is a pause in the flow of the rhythm of a song. The sign ⌢, usually placed above a note, indicates a hold. To conduct a hold, the right arm is extended in front of the body for as long as the hold lasts. Then, a release is given by a preparatory downbeat, and the regular conducting movements for the song are continued.

THE LEFT HAND

Constant use of the left hand along with the right to mark the rhythm detracts from the appearance of the song leader. The left hand should be kept relaxed at the side when not in use for attacks and releases, for accenting strong beats, or for indicating softness and loudness. For soft singing, it should be lowered with the palm down; for loud singing, raised with the palm up.

Interpretation

Interpretation refers to the manner in which a piece of music is performed. Good interpretation reflects the spirit of the music and heightens its emotional and expressive appeal. A good song leader helps his singers interpret each song in a way that is compatible with the spirit and mood of the song. Tempo, dynamics, and phrasing are factors the song leader must consider in interpreting songs.

TEMPO

Tempo refers to the speed of a song. The proper tempo depends principally upon the nature of the song and its expressive intentions. Sentimental songs usually move at a slow tempo, marches and hymns at a moderate tempo, and gay, lilting songs at a fast tempo.

In most community song books, the tempo is indicated in English, but Italian words are used occasionally. The most common Italian terms are: *allegro* (fast), *adagio* (slow), *lento* (slow), *andante* (moderately slow), *moderato* (moderately fast), *accelerando* or *acc.* (gradually faster), *ritard* or *rit.* (gradually slower), and *tenuto* or ⌢ (hold).

In setting a tempo, moderation is the best rule. For a fast song, err on the side of slowness; for a slow, sentimental song, err on the fast side. The tendency of a large group is to sing increasingly slowly. The song leader must set a good tempo and, by his beat, keep the group from dragging. For lively music, use a sharp decisive beat; for patriotic music, use a strong vigorous beat; for quiet, sentimental music, use a smooth, flowing beat.

DYNAMICS

Dynamics refers to the degrees of volume of tones and to the gradual shadings or changes in the volume. Loudness and softness are relative, not absolute, qualities; a tone is soft or loud only in relation to other tones. Contrast in dynamics is one of the most effective and expressive qualities of musical performance.

Most groups of singers tend to sing at the same dynamic level, and miss the thrill inherent in dynamic variety and contrast. The song leader must observe the dynamic markings of a song, decide on the desirable dynamic effects, and, by his conducting, communicate them to the singers. For loud singing, a large beat is used;

for soft singing, a small beat. To indicate gradually louder singing, the size of the beat is increased, and the left hand raised with the palm up. To indicate gradually softer singing, the size of the beat is decreased, and the left hand lowered with the palm down.

The song leader needs to know the common markings for dynamics: *pp* or *pianissimo* (very soft), *p* or *piano* (soft), *mp* or *mezzo piano* (moderately soft), *f* or *forte* (loud), *mf* or *mezzo forte* (moderately loud), *ff* or *fortissimo* (very loud), *crescendo*, *cresc.*, or < (gradually louder), and *diminuendo*, *dim.*, or > (gradually softer).

PHRASING

Music is divided into phrases. A phrase is the shortest meaningful unit in music and can be from three to eight measures in length. The end of a phrase is marked by a pause in the flow of the music, called a cadence. In most songs used for community singing, the musical phrases coincide with the meaning of the words, and the song leader can usually rely on the meaning of the words to indicate the musical phrasing. Phrases are the punctuation of music. Singers usually take a breath at the end of a phrase.

A musical phrase should begin on the dynamic level indicated, gain in intensity and volume to the high point of the phrase, then drop in intensity and volume to the end of the phrase. The song leader indicates the phrasing he desires by increasing the size of the beat to the top of the phrase and by decreasing the size of the beat toward the end of the phrase. A slight *ritard* (slowing down) is effective at the end of the last phrase of a song.

GUIDES FOR PLANNING A SING

The success of a sing depends more on the choice of songs than on any other single factor. No standard selection of songs will suit every occasion. The song leader must exercise intelligence, initiative, and originality in planning his program and must adapt his selection of songs to the preferences of the group he is going to lead. The following instructions will guide the song leader in planning his sing:

1. *Select the major portion of the program from songs that the members of the group are likely to know.* People like to sing songs they know. Everyone knows a few of the old favorite community songs. It is particularly important that the first songs in the program be familiar to the group. Beginning with an unfamiliar song immediately dampens the enthusiasm of the group. Get the singing off to a good start with familiar songs, and the group will then be ready and willing to learn new ones. After one new song, return to familiar songs, and always end the sing with songs they all know.

2. *Select songs that give unity to the program.* An excellent way to achieve unity is to build the program around a central theme, for example, Christmas, Thanksgiving, or one of the other holidays; a section of the country; a foreign country; an occupation; a racial group; or a period in history. Examples of programs built around a central theme appear below:

CHRISTMAS AROUND THE WORLD

England—*The First Noël*
Wales—*Deck the Halls*
France—*Bring a Torch, Jeanette Isabella*
Catalonia—*Fum, Fum, Fum*
Puerto Rico—*To Bethlehem Singing*
Germany—*In Dulci Jubilo*

SONGS FROM ALL OVER AMERICA

Cowboy Songs—*The Old Chisholm Trail* and *Goodbye Old Paint*
Mountain Songs—*Kemo Kimo* and *Sourwood Mountain*
Negro Songs—*Balm in Gilead* and *Shortnin' Bread*
Work Songs—*Erie Canal* and *I've Been Workin' on the Railroad*

SONGS FROM AMERICAN WARS

American Revolution—*Yankee Doodle* and *Hail Columbia*
Civil War—*When Johnny Comes Marching Home* and *Tramp, Tramp, Tramp*
World War I—*There's a Long, Long Trail* and *Over There*

World War II—*Coming in on a Wing and a Prayer, Stage Door Canteen,* and *God Bless America*

SONGS OF LOVE FROM MANY LANDS

Ireland—*Believe Me, If All Those Endearing Young Charms*
England—*The Turtle Dove*
Czechoslovakia—*Walking at Night*
Italy—*Marianina*
Mexico—*Cielito Lindo*
Chile—*River River*
United States—*Let Me Call You Sweetheart*

SONGS OF HOME

Brahms' *Lullaby*
The Ash Grove
I'll Take You Home Again, Kathleen
Home on the Range
On the Banks of the Wabash
Carry Me Back to Old Virginny
Red River Valley

3. *Select songs that give variety to the program.* No two songs on a program should be just alike. With so many good songs available, variety is a simple matter. In seeking variety, consider the mood, the type, the source, the style, the tempo, and the rhythm. Some of the songs should be spirited and gay; others should be quiet and sentimental. Sing a few folk songs and a few composed songs. Sing American songs and songs from foreign countries. Sing songs in unison, songs in parts, and rounds. Sing fast songs and slow songs. Sing songs in waltz rhythm and songs in march rhythm.

4. *Select songs that are compatible with the musical tastes of the group.* The job of the song leader is to give people an opportunity to enjoy singing. He does not accomplish it by selecting songs either too far above or below their level of taste. He may be able gradually to raise the level by skillful introduction of songs of a better type, but a hasty and unsympathetic attempt to do so can only result in the failure of the sing.

5. *Consider the composition of the group.* If the group is com-

posed of a particular age group, choose songs that appeal to that age. Children usually like stirring songs, martial songs, and play songs. Sentimental songs ordinarily do not appeal to them. Adolescents like to sing currently popular songs. Adults usually like to sing sentimental songs and songs that were popular in their youth, but seldom are carried away with action songs.

If the group is all male, give rousing, virile songs, such as work songs, martial songs, and songs good for "barber-shop" singing. If it is female, choose sentimental songs, lullabys, and other songs of a gentle nature.

6. *Select songs compatible with the occasion.* If a holiday or special event is near, sing some songs in commemoration of it. If the weather is unusual or striking, sing a song about it. If a member of the group has had a birthday, mark it with a song. If members of the group have become engaged, have recently been married, or have recently become parents, sing an appropriate song.

7. *Select at least one patriotic song for the beginning or end of the program.* Everyone likes to sing patriotic songs and gets a thrill from singing them with a group. They are effective for building national morale and for developing national unity. Extend the patriotic beyond *America, The Star Spangled Banner,* and *America, the Beautiful.* Many other excellent patriotic songs are often sadly neglected.

8. *Select some songs that are indigenous to where members of the group live or areas from which they have come.* Songs are an important cultural heritage, and people like to sing songs that are part of their culture. For example, if a large number of the singers are from the Southwest, the South, or the far West, sing a few folk songs from that area. If many of the group are descendants of one nationality, sing some of the songs of that nation.

9. *Have some extra songs ready and be prepared to improvise, if the program as planned does not go over with the group.* Occasionally, the best-laid plans come to naught. The mood and temper of the group may be such that the planned program is inappropriate. If the planned program is not going well, do not hesitate

to discard it. Capitalize on the mood and desires of the group, and improvise a new program on the spur of the moment.

10. *Leave some time in the program for songs that members of the group suggest.* The singers feel much more a part of the program if they are given an opportunity to suggest songs. The song leader can still maintain control of the situation by accepting only suggestions of songs which he knows. If someone insists upon a song that the leader does not know, he can ask the person who suggests it to come up and lead it.

11. *If the group is heterogeneous, and the members are not well acquainted with each other, open the singing with an ice-breaker or a get-acquainted song.* People who do not know each other are inclined to be stiff and formal. Good community singing requires informality and friendliness among the singers. An action song, or a song in which the singers all shake hands, often succeeds in breaking the ice.

12. *Choose a key for each song that will place the melody within the range of the majority of the voices.* A key that is too high results in tiring the voices and limits participation. It also causes many of the men to sing the melody two octaves below the sopranos, with unfortunate effect. In many song books, the songs are arranged with the melody in the soprano. If this is the case, and basses and baritones are singing the melody, lower the key an interval of a second or third. For example, *The Star Spangled Banner* is often written in the key of B-flat, and the melody is far beyond the range of most of the men and many of the women. Transposing the song to the key of A-flat helps to remedy the situation.

13. *Bring good-natured competition into the singing.* Pitting one group against another is an effective way of promoting singing through competition. If the group is mixed, ask the women to sing one stanza, the men the second, and all to join in the chorus. The singers may be grouped by seating section, age, geographical origin, color of hair, and other appropriate and amusing standards.

14. *Have a good soloist or special group of singers to partici-*

pate in the sing. A soloist is particularly effective for sea chanteys and spirituals which are often arranged for a solo verse and the group to join in the chorus. The soloist may be an outsider or a member of the group. Always rehearse with him before the sing.

An electrifying effect may be secured by having a group of sopranos sing a descant to a song. A descant is a countermelody which complements and harmonizes with the melody. Rehearse the descant group carefully before the sing and bring them in unannounced on the last stanza of the song, for a glorious and thrilling climax. The descant to *America the Beautiful* in *Singing America* (C. C. Birchard and Co., Boston) is especially lovely. A list of other songs with descants appears on pages 118–119.

15. *Give attention to special abilities within the group.* Almost every group of singers has one or more members with special talent, a vocal or instrumental soloist, or an ensemble of some sort. Use the special talent for a solo, for an unusual accompaniment to the singing, or for a specialty number, such as a skit, a humorous dramatization, or a pantomime of one of the songs.

16. *Plan the accompaniments to the singing.* Always arrange for a competent accompanist and rehearse with him all the songs that he is expected to play. Devise a system of communication with him so that he will know just what you want him to do.

In addition, occasionally use some unusual accompaniment. Instruments like the violin, the trumpet, or the clarinet combine well with the piano or other harmony-playing instruments.

17. *Have all the materials for the sing on hand and well organized.* If song books or song sheets are being used, make prior arrangements for having them distributed and collected. If song slides are used, be sure that the projector is in good working order, that a suitable screen is on hand, and that a competent operator is available. Check to determine that the room can be darkened sufficiently for the singers to read the words on the screen.

18. *Plan the program to run slightly under, rather than over, the time allotted.* An overlong program of singing becomes monotonous and tiresome. Always close the singing while enthusiasm

is at a high pitch. At the slightest sign of diminishing interest, start a rousing song for a finale and resist the temptation to continue.

19. *Plan to wear appropriate clothing for the sing.* Informality is one of the fine characteristics of community singing. The clothing of the song leader should be of the most informal type compatible with the occasion. A jacket and tie are inappropriate for a camp sing, and sports clothes are inappropriate for a more formal sing. Dress as much like the singers as possible. If the women are wearing street dress and the men business suits, wear a conservative business suit. If they are wearing sports clothes or camp clothes, wear clothing of the same type.

PROCEDURES FOR A SING

This portion of the chapter is concerned with the actual singing situation and with specific procedures in which the song leader needs competence in leading a familiar song, an unfamiliar song, a round, an action song, combined songs, unaccompanied singing, and part singing.

Before a person attempts to lead community singing, he must be well prepared and confident of his ability successfully to do the job. He must have practiced the conducting beats until they are natural and easy for him and must have perfected his conducting technique for attacks, releases, and interpretation. He should have planned his program carefully and memorized all the songs he plans to use. He should have rehearsed with his accompanist and with a small group of singers to insure that his conducting movements convey the desired meaning. He should have organized the physical situation properly, with an elevated position for himself, the accompanist close to him, and the singers facing in his direction. Suggestions for procedure for the actual singing follow.

Leading a Familiar Song

The song leader should announce the name and page number of the song and give the group sufficient time to find it. If desired, he may make a few pertinent remarks about the song and the way it should be sung, but should avoid a lengthy discourse. When the group is ready to sing, he signals the accompanist to strike a chord or play a short introduction, and begins the singing.

Once the singing has begun, it is unwise to stop it, unless the situation becomes hopelessly confused. If this should happen, the song leader must keep his temper and his wits about him, interrupt the song with good humor, point out and explain the difficulty, and begin again. Minor flaws are not sufficient reason for interrupting the singing. Nothing is more detrimental to good community singing than the "stop-and-go" approach.

The song leader must exercise his own discretion and good judgment in determining how many times to sing a song and how many stanzas to sing. After the song has been sung once, both the song leader and the group may feel dissatisfied with the performance and want to sing it again. It is desirable for the group to feel a sense of satisfaction after each song, but the singing period must by no means be turned into a choral rehearsal. If a group sings a song twice and the singing still leaves much to be desired, the leader had better move on to an easier song of different type and come back later to the song that proved difficult. With experience, he learns to sense the feeling of the group and can accurately gauge the proper time to move on to something new.

Presenting an Unfamiliar Song

It is absolutely essential that a song leader be able to present an unfamiliar song and teach it to the group with the greatest possible dispatch. If the song is short and simple, he can teach it by rote, but, for most songs, the group needs access to the words by means of song books, song slides, or song sheets.

TEACHING A SONG BY ROTE

To teach a song by rote means to teach both words and music to a group that has access to neither, by singing the song and intoning the words. Only songs that are short and simple enough to be grasped by the group in a few hearings should be taught by rote. Teaching a long and difficult song by rote requires so much time that it is almost impossible to hold the attention of a group assembled for singing. A good procedure for teaching a song by rote follows:

First, the leader sings the song through from the beginning. Next, he asks the singers to sing along with him the second time through, singing "la la" if they cannot remember the words. If the group has difficulty with the words, the leader recites them in rhythm and asks the group to join in. He breaks the song into phrases, sings each phrase, then has the group sing it. After this has been done, he has them sing the entire song. If the group is uncertain about any part of the song, or makes errors in singing, he has them go over the part in question and rehearses the group on it.

TEACHING WHEN THE GROUP HAS THE WORDS

First, the leader sings the entire song while the group listens and follows the words. Next, he sings the first phrase and asks the group to sing it. He proceeds through the song, phrase by phrase, in this manner, and then has the group sing the entire song. If the group has difficulty singing any part of the song, he sings the phrase in which the difficulty occurs and drills the group on it. Rhythmic difficulties may be overcome by his reciting the words in rhythm and having the group recite them. Slight errors should be ignored, but major errors corrected before they become habitual. In case the song leader is unable to sing the song alone satisfactorily, he may use another soloist or a recording of the song.

Leading a Round

If the round is unfamiliar, it should be taught in the usual manner. Most rounds are short enough for teaching by rote. In any case, the group should sing the round in unison before singing it in parts. After the singers have demonstrated that they can sing the round in unison, they should be divided properly into numbered sections which run from front to back. It is important that everyone in the group know in which section he belongs, the order in which the sections are to begin singing, and the number of times the round is to be sung.

The leader should face the first section, start it singing, and sing with it. He then faces each section in turn, as their time to begin singing arrives, and sings with each section on its first entrance. When all sections are singing, he marks the rhythm, being sure to use a steady, definite beat to keep all sections singing in the same tempo. When it is time for each section to cease singing, he signals them with a cut-off. Rounds are always unaccompanied.

Leading an Action Song

If an action song is unfamiliar to the group, it should be taught in the usual manner, but with the actions demonstrated while singing, and without a lengthy description of them. After the group knows the song and understands the actions, the song is started in the usual manner. After the song is started, the leader should discontinue conducting and participate in the actions with enthusiasm.

Leading Combined Songs or Vocal Combats

The group should be divided into two equal parts and each group rehearsed separately, unless the songs are very familiar. Some combined songs start exactly together and present no special problems, but, in some cases, one of the songs starts a beat or two ahead of the other. In the latter situation, it should be pointed out as to which group begins singing first, and the second group should be brought in at the proper time, by conducting. Combined songs are always sung without accompaniment and in unison, because the harmonies of the two songs do not usually coincide.

Leading Unaccompanied Singing

A song leader is often called on to lead singing when there is no means of accompaniment available. Most songs are singable without accompaniment, and many songs with full harmony are most effective when sung without accompaniment.

For unaccompanied singing by the average group, songs chosen should be simple, melodically, harmonically, and rhythmically, and should also be familiar to the group. The leader gets the pitch by ear or with a pitch pipe. (Getting it by ear is preferable, but, if there is any doubt about the ability to hear a satisfactory pitch, there need be no hesitation about using a pitch pipe. The song leader should learn to operate it efficiently and unobtrusively.) The pitch should be relayed to the group by singing the first phrase of the song or by singing the chord on which the song begins. It is a decided risk to sing only the beginning pitch or to depend on the singers getting the pitch from the pitch pipe. The usual result of either of these procedures is that everyone in the group has a different pitch or no pitch at all.

After the pitch is established, leading unaccompanied singing is much the same as leading accompanied singing, except that the leader has to sing with the group most of the time.

Leading Part Singing

Community singing may be in unison, or in two, three, four, or more parts. Although some songs, such as art songs, are written for unison singing, singing in parts greatly enhances the effectiveness and pleasure of singing most types of songs.

One of the responsibilities of the song leader is to encourage singing in parts and to show the singers how to sing parts. Rounds and combined songs are an effective introduction to part singing. After a group has enjoyed hearing the harmony in a round, it usually is ready to learn to sing parts on other songs. For groups inexperienced in part singing, the leader should choose a few songs with simple harmony, like *Home on the Range, Goodnight Ladies,* or *Old Folks at Home,* and emphasize singing parts by ear. The sopranos should sing the melody. It should be demonstrated to the basses how they can sing their part to these songs by singing only three different notes—the first, fourth, and fifth degrees of the scale. The tenors should be shown how to get their part by singing at an interval of a sixth below the melody; and the altos, how to fill in the harmony by singing a tone of the chord between the sopranos and the tenors. The leader should sing with each group in turn until the members can carry on alone.

A quartet of good singers is a great help in developing part singing. They can either stand on the platform with the song leader or go down and mingle with the singers. The accompanist can also help by playing a good firm harmonic accompaniment and by emphasizing each part in turn.

The most effective part singing is possible when the singers are seated according to vocal parts. Although this may be too formal and artificial an arrangement for some community singing, groups which sing together regularly can be so seated. The superior results are well worth the small trouble involved.

Mixed community singing groups preferably sing in four parts (soprano, alto, tenor, and bass). They may also sing in three parts (soprano, alto, and baritone) or in two parts (soprano and baritone). Female groups may sing in two parts (soprano and alto), three parts (soprano, second soprano, and alto), and, occasionally, in four parts (first soprano, second soprano, first alto, and second alto). Three-part singing is customary. Male groups may sing in two parts (tenor and bass), three parts (tenor, baritone, and bass), and, preferably, in four parts (first tenor, second tenor, baritone, and bass).

The song leader should be satisfied with less than perfection in part singing by community singing groups, and should not over-emphasize perfection. Rigorous rehearsal on parts is appropriate for choral singing, but not for community singing.

REPERTORY FOR THE
SONG LEADER

A large and varied repertory of songs is a great asset for the song leader. Without such a repertory he cannot plan and execute interesting and challenging programs of community singing. In building a repertory, he needs to select twenty-five or thirty songs of different types and varied moods, and to memorize them for use on occasions where no song book is available. In addition, he should learn a large number of songs sufficiently well to lead them from a song book, and try to add a new song to the repertory every week. It is well to examine the repertory critically from time to time to make certain that all types of songs are included and that no one type dominates the repertory.

There follows an extended list of songs, all of which have been used successfully in community singing. The list is designed to serve as a guide to the inexperienced song leader in building his repertory. The organization of the list is by type of song. Action songs, art songs, combined songs, folk songs, hymns and chorales, popular songs, rounds, songs with descants, spirituals, and work songs are included. Songs are listed under the names of the song books in which they appear. The song books cited are listed below. Needless to say, these song books do not represent the only sources for the songs.

The Golden Book of Favorite Songs. Hall and McCreary Co.
The "Everybody Sing" Book. Paull-Pioneer Music Corp.
The Gray Book of Favorite Songs. Hall and McCreary Co.
Keep On Singing. Paull-Pioneer Music Corp.
The New American Song Book. Hall and McCreary Co.
Rounds and Canons. Hall and McCreary Co.
Sing! C. C. Birchard and Co.
Sing Along with Harry Wilson. J. J. Robbins and Sons, Inc.
Singing America. C. C. Birchard and Co.
Sociability Songs. The Rodeheaver Co.
Songs We Sing. Hall and McCreary Co.

ACTION SONGS

    The Golden Book of Favorite Songs
        A Gymnastic Relief
        How D'Ye Do?
    Sing!
        Alouette

Howdy
Smile
Sing Along with Harry Wilson
Alouette
The Commuters' Song
Little Tom Tinker
She'll Be Comin' 'Round the Mountain
Sweetly Sings the Donkey
Songs We Sing
Alouette
The Donkey
Hello! Hello!
Little Tom Tinker
Man's Life's a Vapor

ART SONGS

Keep On Singing
Beethoven—Hymn to Joy
Bohm—Calm as the Night
Brahms—The Little Sandman
           Lullaby
Dvořák—Songs My Mother Taught Me
Franz—Dedication
Grieg—I Love Thee
Handel—Where'er You Walk
Humperdinck—Children's Prayer
Mozart—Lullaby
Purcell—Passing By
Schubert—Who Is Sylvia?
Schumann—The Lotus Flower
Sing!
Brahms—Cradle Song
Purcell—Passing By
Schubert—The Boy and the Rose
           Who Is Sylvia?
Silcher—The Loreley
Sing Along with Harry Wilson
Brahms—The Little Sandman
Humperdinck—Evening Prayer *from* Hansel and Gretel
Schubert—The Linden Tree
Wagner—Awake! *from* Die Meistersinger

Singing America
    Brahms—In Wood Embower'd
    Humperdinck—Prayer *from* Hansel and Gretel
    Mozart—Such Chiming Melodious
    Wagner—Awake! *from* Die Meistersinger

COMBINED SONGS OR VOCAL COMBATS

The Golden Book of Favorite Songs
    Darling Nelly Gray *and* When You and I Were Young
    Keep the Home Fires Burning *and* The Long, Long Trail
    Solomon Levi *and* The Spanish Cavalier
    Three Blind Mice *and* Are You Sleeping? (Frère Jacques)
The Gray Book of Favorite Songs
    Ring, Ring the Banjo *and* The Girl I Left behind Me

FOLK SONGS

Grouped by nationality in order to simplify program making.

The "Everybody Sing" Book
    AMERICAN
      Down in the Valley
      Good Bye, My Lover, Good Bye
      Home on the Range
      Little Mohee
      Li'l Liza Jane
      Red River Valley
      She'll Be Comin' 'Round the Mountain
    CREOLE
      Ay, Ay, Ay
    MEXICAN
      Cielito Lindo
      La Cucuracha
    SCOTCH
      Auld Lang Syne
Keep On Singing
    AMERICAN
      Git on Board, Little Chillen
      Listen to the Lambs
      Little David, Play on Your Harp
      Little Mohee
      Rio Grande
      Wide Missouri

AUSTRIAN
   Viennese Lullaby
CZECHOSLOVAKIAN
   At Break of Day
ENGLISH
   Begone, Dull Care
   John Peel
   O No, John
   When Love Is Kind
ESTHONIAN
   Come, My Dear One
FRENCH
   At Pierrot's Door (Au Clair de la Lune)
   Bring a Torch, Jeanette Isabella
   March of the Kings
GERMAN
   Good Night
   Spin, Spin
IRISH
   Bendemeer's Stream
   Tender Apple Blossom
RUSSIAN
   Birch Tree
   Volga Boatmen's Song
SCOTCH
   Charlie Is My Darlin'
WELSH
   The Ash-Grove
The New American Song Book
AMERICAN
   Billy Boy
   The Dying Cowboy
   Hiawatha's Wooing
   Home on the Range
   Li'l Liza Jane
   The Old Chisholm Trail
   Sourwood Mountain
   Whoopie Ti Yi Yo, Git Along, Little Dogies
CREOLE
   Ay, Ay, Ay
   Caroline

CZECHOSLOVAKIAN
  Hymn of the Slavs
  Where Is My Home
ENGLISH
  Drink to Me Only with Thine Eyes
  O, No, John
FRENCH
  Au Clair de la Lune (At Pierrot's Door)
GERMAN
  O Christmas Pine
  Sleep, Baby, Sleep
IRISH
  Believe Me, If All Those Endearing Young Charms
  The Low-Backed Car
  Wearing of the Green
ITALIAN
  Santa Lucia
MEXICAN
  Beautiful Heaven
  The Blue Dove
  Carmela
DUTCH
  The Little Dustman
  Prayer of Thanksgiving
  Rosa
RUSSIAN
  Volga Boatmen
SCOTCH
  Auld Lang Syne
SOUTH AMERICAN
  Chilean Dance Song
  Lullaby
  Morena
  The Pearl
  The River
  There's a Pretty Girl in the Ring
WELSH
  The Ash Grove
  All through the Night
  March of the Men of Harlech

Sing!

AMERICAN
- The Arkansaw Traveler
- The Erie Canal
- Good Bye, Old Paint
- Good Bye, My Lover, Good Bye
- Home on the Range
- The Old Chisholm Trail
- She'll Be Comin' 'Round the Mountain
- Shortnin' Bread
- Water Boy

FRENCH
- Au Clair de la Lune

GERMAN
- Home Song

MEXICAN
- Cielito Lindo

RUSSIAN
- Brown Eyes
- Mother Volga

SOUTH AMERICAN
- Flowing River

Sing Along with Harry Wilson

AMERICAN
- Down in the Valley
- Home on the Range
- Lonesome Road
- The Lone Prairie
- Red River Valley
- She'll Be Comin' 'Round the Mountain
- Shortnin' Bread

CZECHOSLOVAKIAN
- Morning Comes Stealing
- Waters Ripple and Flow
- Stodola Pumpa

ENGLISH
- Drink to Me Only with Thine Eyes
- When Love Is Kind

GERMAN
- In Stilly Night

IRISH
> Believe Me, If All Those Endearing Young Charms
> Londonderry Air
> The Low-Backed Car

MEXICAN
> Chiapanecas
> La Cucuracha

RUSSIAN
> Dark Eyes
> The Pedlar

SCOTCH
> Charlie Is My Darlin'

SOUTH AMERICAN
> River, River

WELSH
> All through the Night

Singing America

AMERICAN
> Night Herding Song
> The Old Chisholm Trail
> Red River Valley
> Shuckin' of the Corn
> Sourwood Mountain
> Wayfaring Stranger

CZECHOSLOVAKIAN
> Walking at Night

ENGLISH
> The Turtle Dove

IRISH
> Believe Me, If All Those Endearing Young Charms
> Bendemeer's Stream

ITALIAN
> Marianina

MEXICAN
> Cielito Lindo

RUSSIAN
> The Pedlar

SOUTH AMERICAN
> Flowing River

Songs We Sing

AMERICAN
  Home on the Range
  Kemo Kimo
  Shortnin' Bread
  Sourwood Mountain

CREOLE
  Ay, Ay, Ay

CZECHOSLOVAKIAN
  Spring Morning

ENGLISH
  Early One Morning
  The Keys of Heaven
  Robin Hood and Little John

ITALIAN
  Morning

DUTCH
  Prayer of Thanksgiving

RUSSIAN
  Pretty Minka
  The Troika

SCOTCH
  Loch Lomond

WELSH
  The Ash Grove

HYMNS AND CHORALES

The "Everybody Sing" Book
  Adeste Fideles
  Battle Hymn of the Republic
  Blest Be the Tie That Binds
  Come Thou, Almighty King
  Holy, Holy, Holy

Keep On Singing
  Break Forth, O Beauteous, Heavenly Light
  Children's Prayer
  Hymn to Joy
  Prayer of Thanksgiving
  Spacious Firmament on High
  Ye Watchers and Ye Holy Ones

The New American Song Book
  Abide with Me
  Blest Be the Tie That Binds
  Faith of Our Fathers
  Lord of All Being
  Now the Day Is Over
  Onward, Christian Soldiers
Sing!
  Abide with Me
  Adeste Fideles
  Blest Be the Tie That Binds
  Come, Thou Almighty King
  Fairest Lord Jesus
  Lead, Kindly Light
  Onward, Christian Soldiers
  Ye Watchers and Ye Holy Ones
Sing Along with Harry Wilson
  Abide with Me
  Christ, the Lord, Is Risen Today
  Dear Lord and Father of Mankind
  Fairest Lord Jesus
  Holy, Holy, Holy
  Now the Day Is Over
  O Sacred Head Now Wounded
  Spirit of God, Descend upon My Heart
Singing America
  Alleluia
  Now All the Woods
  Sing We Now
Songs We Sing
  Adeste Fidelis
  Christ, the Lord, Is Risen Today
  Come, Ye Thankful People
  Fairest Lord Jesus
  For the Beauty of the Earth
  God of Our Fathers
  Joy to the World
  The Little Brown Church in the Vale
  A Mighty Fortress Is Our God
  Now the Day Is Over

Onward, Christian Soldiers
The Spacious Firmament on High

POPULAR SONGS

These are a few good hit tunes from the past. Most recent hit tunes are still under copyright and do not normally appear in community songbooks. They can be secured in sheet music.

The "Everybody Sing" Book
   The Bowery
   Ciribiribin
   Daisy Bell
   If I Had My Way
   Let Me Call You Sweetheart
   Little Annie Rooney
   The Merry Widow Waltz
   On the Banks of the Wabash
   The Rose of Tralee
   The Sidewalks of New York
   Vilia
Sing Along with Harry Wilson
   The Band Played On
   Clementine
   Daisy Bell
   Little Annie Rooney
   The Man on the Flying Trapeze
   Ta-ra-ra Boom De-Ay
Sing!
   Listen to the Mocking Bird
   Little Annie Rooney

ROUNDS

The "Everybody Sing" Book
   Are You Sleeping?
   Good Night to You All
   Lovely Evening
   Man's Life's a Vapor
   Where Is John?
The New American Song Book
   Good Night
   Scotland's Burning

Sing Along with Harry Wilson
  Dona Nobis Pacem
  Good Night to You All
  Little Tom Tinker
  Lovely Evening
  Row, Row, Row Your Boat
  Sing Together
  Sweetly Sings the Donkey
Rounds and Canons
  Are You Sleeping?
  Christmas Is Coming
  Day Is Done
  The Donkey
  Ducks on a Pond
  Good Night
  Health and Strength
  Lovely Evening
  Man's Life's a Vapor
  My Goose
  Little Tom Tinker
  Now Comes the Hour
  The Orchestra
  Row, Row, Row Your Boat
  Three Blind Mice

SONGS WITH DESCANTS

Sing!
  Fairest Lord Jesus
  Home on the Range
  Three Kings of Orient
  Ye Watchers and Ye Holy Ones
Sing Along with Harry Wilson
  Christ, the Lord, Is Risen Today
  O God, Our Help in Ages Past
  O Little Town of Bethlehem
  Silent Night
  Spirit of God, Descend upon My Heart
  We Three Kings of Orient Are
Singing America
  Alleluia
  America, the Beautiful

At the Gate of Heaven
Believe Me, If All Those Endearing Young Charms
Christmas Spring
Old Folks at Home
Songs We Sing
Adeste Fidelis
America, the Beautiful
Boll Weevil
Christ, the Lord, Is Risen Today
Come, Ye Thankful People
Fairest Lord Jesus
For the Beauty of the Earth
In the Evening by the Moonlight
Joy to the World
Loch Lomond
Now the Day Is Over
O Come, All Ye Faithful
Onward, Christian Soldiers
The Rose of Tralee
Silent Night

SPIRITUALS

The "Everybody Sing" Book
Deep River
Go Down, Moses
Nobody Knows the Trouble I See
Standin' in the Need of Prayer
Swing Low, Sweet Chariot
Steal Away
Keep On Singing
Battle of Jericho
Git on Board, Little Chillen
Listen to the Lambs
Little David, Play on Your Harp
Old Ark's A-Moverin' Along
The New American Song Book
Couldn't Hear Nobody Pray
Deep River
It's a-Me, O Lord
I Want to Be Ready
Nobody Knows the Trouble I See

Old Ark's A-Moverin' Along
Steal Away
Swing Low, Sweet Chariot
Sing!
    Balm in Gilead
    Every Time I Feel de Spirit
Sing Along with Harry Wilson
    Cotton Needs Pickin'
    Git on Board
    Go Down, Moses
    Go Tell It on the Mountain
    Heav'n, Heav'n
    Jacob's Ladder
    Swing Low, Sweet Chariot
    Were You There?
Singing America
    Jacob's Ladder
    Listen to the Lambs
    Lord, I Want to Be a Christian
    My Lord, What a Mornin'
Songs We Sing
    Deep River
    I Ain't Gonna Grieve My Lord No More
    Keep in the Middle of the Road
    Swing Low, Sweet Chariot
    Won't You Sit Down?

WORK SONGS

The "Everybody Sing" Book
    Blow the Man Down
    I've Been Workin' on the Railroad
    Rio Grande
    Sailing
The New American Song Book
    Blow the Man Down
    The Erie Canal
    Levee Song
    Nancy Lee
Sing!
    The Erie Canal
    Heave Away, My Johnnie

Mother Volga
Shenandoah
Sing Along with Harry Wilson
Blow the Man Down
The Erie Canal
I've Been Workin' on the Railroad
Singing America
Rio Grande
Sacramento
Shenandoah
Songs We Sing
Blow the Man Down
The Erie Canal

CHAPTER SIX

RECREATION

THROUGH PLAYING

Throughout history, myriads of people have played instruments for recreation purposes. Before the advent of the phonograph, radio, and television, almost every family had one or more members who played an instrument. The piano was the most valuable object in the home, and many families possessed and played several other instruments. With the arrival of the mechanical means of producing music, a great hue and cry arose that the day of the active producer of music had passed, and that the mass of people were doomed to become mere consumers of music. To be sure, these mechanical instruments did affect the music customs and habits of the people. Many families sold their pianos to make room for a phonograph or radio, and stored in the attic, or otherwise disposed of, their other musical instruments. The automobile had a further effect of decentralizing the sphere of family recreation, as did moving pictures and other commercial amusements.

As the novelty of all these devices wore off, people became dissatisfied with being passive participants in music. They realized that they were missing the incomparable satisfaction to be gained from making one's own music. They discovered that flipping an electrical switch was no substitute for the satisfaction that self-expression through one's own performance can give. They wanted to participate actively in music.

The increase in the availability of fine music through the radio and phonograph has actually resulted in an increase in personal music-making. During the past few years, pianos and other musical instruments have sold in vastly increased numbers. In fact, instrument makers have often had difficulty in meeting the demand. More and more people want to own an instrument and make music with it.

The public and private schools of the country have exerted a great and salutary influence on the music habits of the people. Instrumental music has gained an important place in the curriculum of the modern elementary and secondary schools. Almost every school has a vital and growing program of instrumental music instruction. Children of all ages are learning to play instruments of all kinds in school, and thousands of school bands and orchestras attain a high artistic standard. Piano and other instrument classes, chamber music groups, dance orchestras, and other activities are part of the school instrumental music program.

The recreation program must meet the desires of the people to play for recreation, and must nurture and develop their talent and capacities. It must also build upon and extend the accomplishments of the schools and other agencies in this direction.

The recreation program for playing instruments has a twofold purpose: (1) to provide an opportunity to learn to play an instrument for persons who have had no such opportunity previously, and (2) to provide a continuing musical experience for persons who have previously received instruction from a private teacher, from the school music program, or from some other source. In order to meet the needs of both of these groups, the recreation music program should offer elementary class instruction in playing instruments and should sponsor the organization of instrumental ensembles.

INSTRUMENTAL CLASSES

Instrumental teaching traditionally has been carried on in private lessons, but private lessons are expensive and have little or no place in an organized recreation program. After participation in a recreation program, many persons may wish to begin private study to improve their facility and further develop their ability. This is a highly desirable outcome, but is not properly within the province of the recreation program.

Over the past few years, there has been tremendous progress

in the development of techniques for teaching instruments in classes. Although class lessons were never intended to replace private lessons for the student on an advanced level, they have several distinct advantages for instruction on an elementary level.

Class lessons take care of many who want to learn, with a reasonable expenditure of time and money on the part of the recreation personnel. With the same amount of instruction time, one instructor can reach many more people than in private lessons, and the cost per person is consequently reduced to a negligible amount.

Class lessons socialize the music lesson. Many people are reluctant to begin private lessons because of shyness and timidity. In the class situation, surrounded by their peers, they approach the learning of a new skill with poise and confidence. During class instruction, the students constantly perform before their fellows, playing alone and ensemble, and they learn by observing others. Many individual problems are common to the whole group and often can be solved for everyone at the same time. Each member feels that he is part of the group and assumes a share of the responsibility for the progress of the class.

The class situation is an excellent means of stimulating and maintaining interest. All people are accustomed to learning with a group, since most organized learning takes place in a group situation. School subjects, games, and other areas are almost always taught in classes. Instrumental music need not be an exception. The element of competition among members of the class stimulates their growth and development. Because of the increased interest and superior motivation resulting from group work, students are much less likely to drop their instrumental study than if pursuing it privately.

The class situation draws on the combined abilities of the instructor and all the students. In private lessons, only the abilities of the instructor and one student are brought into play. The class situation is a much richer and livelier setting for learning. The expression of many ideas and points of view helps to solve both technical and musical problems.

A well qualified instructor can teach all instruments successfully in classes. The most important qualifications of the instructor are competence on the instrument he is teaching, a broad musical background, an interest in recreational music, a sympathetic and understanding attitude toward amateur musicians, and an understanding of and experience with efficient methods of group instrumental instruction.

The size of the class may vary from six to twenty persons. A class smaller than six ceases to be a class and is likely to become no more than a series of short and ineffective private lessons. A class larger than twenty is cumbersome and does not permit the necessary individual attention on the part of the instructor. The optimum size for a class is around fifteen students.

Two hours of class work each week is the minimum amount of time required for good results. Three hours a week would be desirable, but probably cannot be accomplished in a recreation program. The class time is best divided into two sessions each week, but this is seldom possible.

The length of the course depends upon the complexity and the possibilities of the instrument, and may range from a month to a year or more. The average person can learn to play the recorder, the auto-harp, or the ukelele satisfactorily in a month or six weeks. The piano or violin and certain other instruments, on the other hand, can be studied for years with profit and without exhausting the possibilities of the instrument.

A well-organized program of instrumental class instruction can be self-supporting. There need be no hesitation about making a charge for instruction, sufficient to pay the instructor and to defray other expenses. People are inclined to value that for which they pay and to deprecate that which they receive without charge. It is wise to charge fees on a course basis. Under this arrangement, the students are much more likely to finish the course they have begun. The method of payment should be in advance for each course or monthly in advance.

Piano Classes

Since its invention in the early part of the eighteenth century, the piano has been the dominant and most popular of all instruments. Whether an aged upright, a dainty new spinet, or a concert grand, the piano has tremendous expressive possibilities and universal appeal for players and listeners.

The piano is an ideal instrument for the amateur musician. It is complete within itself and encompasses the entire range of musical pitch. It can play melody and harmony at the same time, and its expressive potential is almost limitless. It is incomparable as a solo instrument and for accompanying singing, yet it fits into any combination of instruments playing in an ensemble. There is an endless supply of piano literature on all levels of difficulty. With few exceptions, all the great composers have written piano music.

Numerous studies of recreation choice among adults have shown that playing the piano is a favorite. When asked what skill they wish they had learned but did not learn, a surprising number answer, "I wish I had learned to play the piano."

Anyone who has normal reaction patterns and physical coordination can learn to play the piano. Many people who find it difficult to carry a tune in singing can play the piano with great satisfaction to themselves and others. Because of the fixed mechanical nature of the instrument, fine discriminations in pitch are not absolutely necessary. People of all ages can begin the study of piano profitably.

At least one piano in good tune is the minimum essential for conducting a piano class. It is desirable to have as many pianos in the room as possible, preferably one for each student. If there is only one piano, students alternate in using it and use mechanical silent keyboards the remainder of the time. The keys of a silent keyboard move in much the same way as the keys of the piano. Several excellent silent keyboards are available at a reasonable price and are a satisfactory substitute for multiple pianos. Stationary wooden keyboards or paper keyboards are less expensive and can be used temporarily, but they are much less desirable than the mechanical keyboards. A blackboard with music staves painted on it and an instruction book for each student complete the necessary equipment.

Because of the great demand for piano instruction, there has been perhaps greater progress in the development of instruction books and class-teaching techniques for the piano than for any other instrument. The adult beginner has received special attention. The emphasis in modern piano instruction books is generally on playing simple music by note and by ear rather than on technical drills and exercises.

Students in a piano class must practice outside of class. Without practice between lessons, little can be accomplished. A regular period of thoughtful and careful practice produces the best results. One hour of practice each day is the optimum amount for the amateur player. Much less than an hour daily impedes progress, but much more soon ceases to be recreation and becomes work.

The progress made by the students will naturally vary considerably, but within thirty weeks every student can ordinarily be expected to make sufficient progress to be able to continue on his own or to study with a private teacher if he desires to do so. In some situations, it may be desirable to offer instruction on a more advanced level for those who have completed the elementary course and wish to continue.

Orchestra and Band Instrument Classes

The recreation music program properly includes class instruction in orchestra and band instruments. Although these melody-playing instruments offer recreation when played alone that is somewhat less satisfying than the piano, many people prefer to learn to play them. This is especially true when learning to play leads to participation in a band, orchestra, or some other instrumental ensemble.

The violin, clarinet, and trumpet are generally the most popular instruments, because they are the principal ones in their respective sections and usually carry the lead part in instrumental ensembles. On the other hand, instruments such as the viola, cello, oboe, flute, and trombone also have recreational possibilities and are necessary for the development of well-balanced instrumental groups. Some of the bass instruments, such as the string bass, bassoon, and tuba, offer little satisfaction when played alone, but instruction in these instruments is desirable if the players can look forward to playing in a band or orchestra.

Three types of instrumental classes have proved successful: (1) classes receiving instruction in a single instrument, (2) classes receiving instruction in related instruments, and (3) classes receiving instruction in all instruments. The type of class to be used depends upon the size of the instrumental program and the availability of instructors.

In the first type, separate classes are organized for each instrument. This is efficient and often practicable for the popular instruments, such as violin, clarinet, and trumpet. The students make greater progress this way because of the similarity of the problems involved for each person. On the other hand, it is seldom possible to organize separate classes for the more unusual instruments, such as oboe, bassoon, and string bass, because of the small number of students desiring instruction in these instruments. This type of class is preferable in a large program where sufficiently large classes in each instrument can be organized.

In the second type, several related instruments are taught in one class—for example, all the stringed instruments, or all the wood winds, or all the brasses. The basic problems in playing related instruments are similar and can be solved in one class without great difficulty. In this way, only three classes are required to teach all the instruments, and the instruction is accomplished with much less expense than is possible with separate classes in each instrument. Another advantage is that ensemble playing can be started almost immediately. This type of class is recommended in situations where it is feasible to organize only three classes. It may also be combined with the first type in order to teach the more unusual instruments. For example, separate classes may be offered in violin, clarinet, and trumpet, with the other three stringed instruments in one class, the remainder of the wood winds in one class, and the other brasses in one class.

In the third type of class, where all instruments are taught, the tremendous differences in pitch, timbre, and playing technique make effective instruction difficult. However, many teachers have had considerable success with this type. It is the least expensive of the three types and, when the number of students is small and instruction time limited, it offers a practicable solution to the problem of offering instrumental instruction. The fact that the instruments for a complete orchestra or band are together from the first day of instruction somewhat compensates for the instructional difficulties inherent in the teaching situation and makes the transition to playing in a band or orchestra quite smooth. In fact, such a class often serves as a nucleus for a beginning orchestra or band. Such classes are especially effective when they can meet daily, for example, at a camp.

Instrumental class instruction requires that each member of the class have an instrument. It is preferable for each person to own his instrument, but, if this is impossible, the organization sponsoring the classes may secure instruments and rent or lend them to those who have no instruments.

Aside from the instruments themselves, the equipment requirements for instrumental classes are modest. Straight-back chairs that promote good posture, a blackboard ruled with music staves, music racks, and an instruction book for each student represent the essential items of equipment. A piano, although not absolutely necessary, is useful for tuning instruments, correcting intonation, and playing accompaniments.

Learning to play most orchestral and band instruments requires time and considerable practice. The length of the course varies from ten to thirty weeks, depending upon the time spent in classes and in practice. In situations where daily lessons are possible, such as summer camps, students make astounding progress within a short time. With only one lesson each week, the length of time necessary for attaining elementary skill is naturally increased. Students in instrumental classes make much faster progress if they have immediate opportunity to play in a band, orchestra, or other instrumental group.

Simple Instrument Classes

A number of simple instruments have excellent recreational possibilities and also lend themselves to class instruction. Among them are the banjo, guitar, ukelele, mandolin, ocarina, recorder, autoharp, harmonica, and accordion. These instruments are much less complex than the piano or orchestral and band instruments. Consequently, the period of instruction necessary to learn to play them is significantly shorter. Although their musical possibilities are limited, these instruments offer immediate satisfaction to the player when played alone, in ensembles, or for accompanying singing and dancing. Most of them are inexpensive to purchase, and some of them can easily be made by hand. They are all easily portable and can be available for use in any situation on a moment's notice. Most of these instruments require only a few lessons for the player to perform satisfactorily. They are particularly desirable for children and for adults who have never played an instrument. They offer an excellent point of departure for learning to play the more complex instruments. Descriptions of some of these instruments follow:

FRETTED INSTRUMENTS

Fretted instruments are stringed instruments with raised lines, called frets, which mark the positions for different tones on the fingerboard. These instruments are played by plucking or strumming the strings with the fingers or a pick. They provide a simple chordal accompaniment for singing and dancing.

The Guitar. The guitar has a flat back and inward curving sides. The modern guitar has six strings which are tuned in fourths.

The Banjo. The banjo is a guitar-like instrument, with a long neck and a body in the form of an open drum, and is frequently used in jazz orchestras. Parchment stretched over the body serves as a resonator. It has six strings also.

The Ukelele. The ukelele is a Hawaiian instrument of the guitar family. It has four strings and is the simplest of the fretted instruments.

The Mandolin. The mandolin, the only instrument of the lute family in general use today, is played with a pick made of tortoise shell. A quick, vibrating motion of the pick produces tones in a sustained tremolo. Figures 16, 17, and 18 illustrated the fretted instruments.

MELODY-PLAYING INSTRUMENTS

Most of the simple melody-playing instruments are variations of the whistle flute. They have a whistle mouthpiece at one end through which the player blows to produce the tone.

The Recorder. The recorder (Figure 19), an ancient instrument with a soft reedy tone, has more musical possibilities than other instruments of this type. It was used a great deal in serious music up to the seventeenth century. Although it was virtually forgotten during the eighteenth and nineteenth centuries, interest in it has revived during the present century. The modern recorder, available in four sizes (soprano, alto, tenor, and bass), is widely used for recreational playing, both as a solo instrument and in bands.

The Ocarina. The ocarina (Figure 20), or "sweet potato," is a popular form of whistle flute. It resembles a sweet potato in appearance. It has a mouthpiece and varying number of finger holes. It is easy to play and widely used, especially by children.

Many more variations of the whistle flute are available. Among them are tonettes, melody flutes, toy flutes, and others. They are, in general, inferior to the ocarina, but are inexpensive and have recreational possibilities. Many people make their own flutes from reeds. A. D. Zanzig has written an excellent and informative booklet, *How to Make and Play a Shepherd Pipe*, which may be secured from the National Recreation Association (315 Fourth Avenue, New York).

OTHER SIMPLE INSTRUMENTS

Autoharp. The autoharp (Figure 21), a member of the zither family, has from 30 to 45 strings which the player plucks with two plectrums, or picks, one on the thumb and one on the first finger of the right hand. There is a series of bars, or buttons, one for each common chord. To produce a chord, the player presses one of the bars and plucks the strings with the thumb pick. Depressing the bar damps all the strings except those required for the chord to be played. To play a melody, the player plucks single strings with the first-finger pick. Thus he can play a melody, a chordal accompaniment, or both at the same time. The autoharp is an excellent instrument for accompanying the singing of small groups. Self-teaching instruction books may be secured from Oscar Schmidt-International Inc. (87–101 Ferry Street, Jersey City, N.J.).

Harmonica. The harmonica, or mouth organ, is a small, flat box with a number of holes in the side. Each hole leads to a metal reed inside the box. The player places the instrument against his lips and moves it in one direction or the other to produce the notes he desires. He obtains alternate notes of the scale by blowing or by suction. The harmonica is a good solo instrument, and harmonica bands are numerous and popular in the United States. M. Hohner and Co. (351 Fourth Avenue, New York) gives each purchaser of a Hohner Harmonica a copy of *How to Play the Harmonica*. The Leisure League of America (39 Rockefeller Plaza, New York) publishes *How to Make Music on the Harmonica*.

INSTRUMENTAL
ENSEMBLES

Instrumental ensembles in the recreation program have a two-fold purpose: (1) to provide worth-while recreation for the members of the ensemble, by giving them a continuing, purposeful playing experience, and (2) to furnish a recreational listening experience for other people. In every group of people, there are those who have played musical instruments and who would continue to play them if they had the opportunity to do so. Each year, schools and colleges graduate thousands of young people who have had several years of instrumental instruction and who have played in excellent school and college bands and orchestras. For too many of these young musicians, graduation marks the end of active musical participation. This is a regrettable waste of a rich cultural resource which should be nurtured and saved for the pleasure of the individual and the enrichment of the community. In addition to the people who have played instruments in schools, others have had instrumental instruction from private teachers or have learned to play instruments at home. The introduction of instrumental classes in the recreation program further increases the number of people who desire to play in an instrumental group. The recreation program must utilize these rich human resources, for the good of the individual and society, by organizing appropriate instrumental ensembles.

Many different types of instrumental ensembles are appropriate for a recreation program. They range all the way from symphony orchestras to small groups of simple instruments.

Orchestras

An orchestra may vary in size from six instruments to over a hundred. As described in Chapter 2 there are four sections in an orchestra: strings, wood winds, brasses, and percussions. Strings are the *sine qua non* of an orchestra and usually make up about

60 per cent of the instruments. Balance is important in an orchestra, and the preponderance of strings should be maintained.

A small orchestra may consist of three violins, a trumpet, a clarinet, drums, and a piano. Starting with a group such as this as a nucleus, many orchestras have expanded and developed into fine, large organizations.

For a twenty-eight-piece orchestra, the following instrumentation is suggested: twelve violins, two violas, two cellos, two string basses, one flute, two clarinets, two French horns, two trumpets, one trombone, one tuba, and drums.

For a ninety-eight-piece orchestra, a satisfactory instrumentation would be: twenty first violins, eighteen second violins, twelve violas, ten cellos, ten string basses, three flutes, three oboes, four clarinets, three bassoons, four French horns, four trumpets, three trombones, one tuba, tympani, and drums.

When organizing an orchestra, the person or groups of people in charge should select one of the suggested instrumentations as their goal. When the first goal is reached, they can move gradually toward the larger organization.

There are many excellent community and recreational orchestras throughout the country. In New York, there are many such orchestras, including the Doctors' Orchestra, which is an outstanding organization composed of men in the medical profession who rehearse regularly and give occasional concerts just because they like to play. Flint, Michigan; Reading, Pennsylvania; Summit, New Jersey; and Ottawa, Kansas are a few of the many other cities which have successful community orchestras.

It is interesting to note the variety of ways in which community orchestras have been started. In some cases, the initiative for organizing orchestras has come from the conductor, from a recreation leader, or from a committee of laymen. In some cities, community orchestras have grown out of high school orchestras, with players from the schools serving as a nucleus reinforced by graduates and other townspeople. Other orchestras have been started when a group of players got together, started playing in a small group, and gradually recruited new members.

An orchestra needs regular rehearsals and opportunities for public performance. One 2-hour rehearsal per week is the absolute minimum, and this may need to be supplemented by additional rehearsals before performances. Public performance not only gives a tremendous incentive to the orchestra, but also gains support for the orchestra from the community. Every orchestra should give one major program each year and several shorter programs at appropriate times. In addition to formal concerts, orchestras may participate in the musical life of the community by playing short programs in churches and schools and at club and other appropriate public meetings. They may also play accompaniments for operettas, musical shows, and for community singing.

There is excellent published material for orchestras of all sizes and instrumentations, and every orchestra should own several collections for general use. Orchestras usually rent orchestrations of symphonic works because of their high purchase price.

Readers interested in organizing an orchestra are referred to *Starting and Maintaining a Community Orchestra*, by A. D. Zanzig, a booklet published by the National Recreation Association, 315 Fourth Ave., New York, and to *School Orchestras: How They May Be Developed*, by J. E. Maddy, a booklet published by the National Bureau for the Advancement of Music (315 Fourth Avenue, New York).

Bands

A band is composed of wind instruments and percussions, and contains three sections: wood winds, brasses, and percussions. There are two types of bands: the concert band and the marching band. The concert band contains a preponderance of wood winds and often plays indoors. The marching band emphasizes brasses and percussions in order to attain the volume and brilliance necessary for playing outdoors.

Bands range in size from twenty-one to over a hundred pieces. A band of twenty-one pieces may consist of four clarinets, two saxophones, four cornets, three horns, one baritone horn, three trombones, two tubas and two drums. A typical concert band contains five flutes, twenty-six clarinets, two alto clarinets, two oboes, two bass clarinets, two bassoons, five saxophones, six cornets, four trumpets, two fluegel horns, six French horns, six trombones, four baritone horns, six tubas, tympani, and three drums.

Town bands are an important tradition in the United States. During the past 50 years, school bands have undergone startling development. Professional bands formerly flourished, but with the development of school bands, they are much less numerous.

Bands may be organized in much the same way as orchestras and have the same requirements for rehearsals and public performance. They are easier to develop than orchestras, and the results are more immediate. Bands offer stirring music for parades, rallies, games, and similar events. They may also be used to accompany community singing when the group is large. A band should not be considered a rival of an orchestra, and the organization of one does not preclude the organization of the other. They are different organizations with different purposes and potentialities, and one organization actually complements the other.

School Bands: How They May Be Developed, by J. E. Maddy, a booklet published by the National Bureau for the Advancement of Music, contains comprehensive information on the organization of bands. Much of the material in *Starting and Maintaining a Community Orchestra* is also pertinent to the organization of a band.

Dance Bands

A good dance band can make a big contribution to the recreation program. A dance band not only gives pleasure to the players, but also makes possible the arrangement of frequent and inexpensive social dances.

The instrumentation of a dance band is quite flexible and

ranges from three to sixteen instruments. A piano, banjo, and string bass can provide adequate rhythm for dancing. A good five-piece combination consists of piano, drums, cornet, saxophone, and guitar.

The most popular combinations have from eight to twelve players. A good eight-piece band consists of one tenor and two alto saxophones, one trumpet, one trombone, piano, drums, and string bass. For a ten-piece band, a trumpet and guitar are added. Bands of more than ten pieces frequently have additional wood winds and brasses along with two or three violins to lend color.

Stock arrangements of all the latest popular songs are available at most music stores. They are so arranged that they can be used by a band of any size.

Rhythm Bands

The rhythm band provides an excellent musical and recreational experience for children between the ages of four and twelve. Adolescents and adults occasionally enjoy experience with rhythm instruments in connection with community singing. A rhythm band may consist of only simple percussion instruments, such as triangles, drums, tom-toms, castanets, cymbals, wood blocks, rattles, and clappers. When percussion instruments alone are used, the piano or a phonograph recording furnishes the music. Most of the percussion instruments are easy to make, and children enjoy making their own instruments. With older children in the band, simple melody instruments, such as whistle flutes, ocarinas, shepherd pipes, and harmonicas may be combined with the percussion instruments.

A person who is musically untrained can start a rhythm band with pleasure for himself and the children. *Starting and Developing a Rhythm Band,* by A. D. Zanzig and published by the National Recreation Association, contains comprehensive instructions for the organization of a rhythm band and for making simple instruments.

Other Bands

Accordions, harmonicas, mandolins, guitars, recorders, fifes, drums, and bugles can be combined to organize different kinds of bands. Harmonica bands, recorder bands, fife and drum corps, and bugle corps are the most frequent and popular combinations.

Small Instrumental Ensembles

The recreation program should include small instrumental ensembles of all different kinds of instruments. Small ensembles combine the qualities of solo playing and playing in large ensembles, and give great satisfaction to the players. Because the players work on their own and require no director, these ensembles present few administrative problems.

Small instrumental ensembles range in size from two to twelve players, and consist of instruments of one type or several types. Frequent combinations follow:

STRINGED INSTRUMENTS

Two instruments: violin and piano; viola and piano; cello and piano; two violins; two violas; two cellos; violin and viola; violin and cello; viola and cello.

Three instruments: violin, viola, and cello; violin, viola, and piano (piano trio); three violins, violas, or cellos; two violins and viola or cello; piano and two violins, violas, or cellos.

Four instruments: two violins, viola, and cello (string quartet); violin, viola, cello, and piano (piano quartet); two violins and two violas; two violas and two cellos; two violas, cello, and string bass.

Five instruments: two violins, two violas, and cello (string quintet); any of the four-instrument combinations with an added violin.

Six instruments: two violins, viola, cello, string bass, and piano.

WOOD-WIND INSTRUMENTS

Two instruments: two flutes; two oboes; two clarinets; two bassoons; any two of these instruments; any one of these instruments and piano or English horn.

Three instruments: flute, clarinet, and bassoon; oboe, clarinet, and bassoon; clarinet, oboe, and English horn; oboe, English horn, and bassoon; any two of these instruments and piano.

Four instruments: flute, oboe, clarinet, and bassoon; oboe, clarinet, English horn, and bassoon; any three of these instruments and piano.

BRASS INSTRUMENTS

Two instruments: two trumpets; two horns; two trombones; two baritone horns; any two of these instruments.

Three instruments: any three of the brass instruments.

Four instruments: two trumpets and two horns; two trumpets, horn, and trombone; four trombones.

Five instruments: either of the above quartets with tuba added.

SIMPLE INSTRUMENTS

Harmonicas, mandolins, guitars, banjos, ukeleles, recorders, ocarinas and others, combined with instruments of the same type or with instruments of different types.

CHAPTER SEVEN

THE RECREATION
LEADER AND THE
PLAYING PROGRAM

The recreation leader's relationship to the playing program may differ considerably from his relationship to the listening and singing programs. As has been pointed out, he can participate actively in the listening and singing programs, even if he is an untrained musician. On the other hand, active leadership in the playing program requires the technique and skill of a music specialist. With the exception of organizing a rhythm band, and, perhaps, playing and teaching one or more of the simple instruments, the responsibilities of the recreation leader in the playing program are largely administrative, unless he is a music specialist. In any case, he needs to be concerned with planning the program, securing and maintaining facilities and equipment, selecting competent personnel, organizing and scheduling the program, and integrating the playing program with other phases of the recreation program. A discussion of his administrative functions in the playing program follows.

1. *He stimulates interest in the playing program.* Many persons lack interest in playing instruments, because they think that playing instruments requires unusual talent, and because they assume that playing is beyond their ability. Demonstrating that anybody can learn to play an instrument arouses interest. There are many other ways to stimulate interest. If the recreation leader plays an instrument himself, he may play for the group and tell how he learned to play. If he does not play an instrument, he may arrange for groups to come in contact with amateur players through recitals and demonstrations. This always arouses interest, particu-

larly if the performance is followed by a discussion of the instruments and an opportunity for the listeners to handle the instruments and experiment on them. Bringing in an expert teacher and having him conduct a demonstration class in which he gives inexperienced players their first lesson, is another good idea. Making articles, books, and other literature about recreational playing easily available to the group stimulates interest. Bringing percussion instruments and simple melody-playing instruments into the community singing, for different people to play as accompaniment for the singing, is effective. Such introductory experiences influence many people to want to play instruments.

2. *He determines the needs and interests of the members of the group.* A successful playing program, like all recreation programs, must be built around the needs and interests of those who participate in the program. Before the recreation leader can know what kind of a playing program to organize, he must know a great deal about the musical backgrounds of the people he is serving. He must also know where their interests lie, what their abilities are, and the amount of leisure time at their disposal. For example, it would be impossible to organize a band or orchestra from members of a group who have had no previous instruction in playing instruments, but classes in playing instruments would be possible and desirable and would probably lead eventually to the organization of a band or orchestra. Again, if the members of a group have little time for practice, instruction in simple instruments, such as the guitar or auto-harp, would probably be preferable to piano instruction.

The recreation leader can use several different techniques to determine needs and interests, but the basis for his success is getting to know and understand the members of the group. Private conferences and group discussions are always helpful. The leader should talk individually with several persons who know the situation well and who are leaders in the group, and should arrange a meeting of interested persons to discuss freely the playing program. A short questionnaire, asking each person to indicate the type of activity in which he is interested, may be prepared in the form of a checklist and distributed widely. A suggested form for a questionnaire appears on page 143.

3. *He organizes the playing program.* After the recreation leader has succeeded in arousing interest and has determined the needs and interests of the group, he organizes a playing program that takes into account all that he has learned about the people with whom he is dealing. He should start the program as soon as possible, even if at first only a few activities are included. An active program itself arouses further interest, and the program can be modified and expanded to meet additional needs as circumstances warrant.

The planning and organization of the playing program should be approached in a democratic way. The program gains strength from having a representative body participate in the planning. Provision should be made for the formation of a music committee or music council composed of elected or volunteer representatives of the group. The members of the council should be given as much responsibility as possible, and their ability used for the good of the program. With the assistance of a council, the recreation leader may better develop a program consistent with the needs of the group.

The program should be started where the people are and should insure the playing activities being within the ability of most members of the group. Among the principal reasons for the failure of music programs is the musical experience being beyond the comprehension of the group and the technical aspects of music being overemphasized. If the group lacks musical experience, the leader should begin with classes in simple instruments, pointing toward the organization of ensembles, such as a harmonica band or a recorder band. On the other hand, the potentialities of the group should not be underestimated. Most people dislike being patronized and will not respond to a leader who plays down to them.

The program must offer a continuing and purposeful chal-

QUESTIONNAIRE FOR DETERMINING
INTEREST IN THE PLAYING PROGRAM

We are contemplating organizing an instrumental music program as part of the recreation program. You can assist us in planning the kind of program you desire by filling out this questionnaire.

1. Are you interested in learning to play an instrument? Yes_____. No_____.

2. If the answer is "yes," check the instrument or instruments in which you are most interested: piano_____, violin _____, viola_____, cello_____, flute_____, oboe_____, trumpet_____, trombone_____, French horn_____, guitar_____, mandolin _____, ukelele_____, recorder_____, autoharp _____, ocarina_____.

3. What instrument can you play at this time?_____.

4. If you can play an instrument, check the instrumental ensemble of which you would like to be a member: band_____, orchestra_____, dance band_____, recorder band_____, string ensemble_____, brass ensemble_____, wood-wind ensemble_____, other (specify)_____.

5. Indicate below the hours when you are free to attend instrumental classes or to play in an instrumental ensemble.

Monday_____   Tuesday_____
Wednesday_____   Thursday_____
Friday_____   Saturday_____

DIAGRAM 9

lenge. As the group makes progress, new and rewarding activities should be introduced. Classes in piano and orchestra instruments are a natural outgrowth of classes in simple instruments. The organization of a band or orchestra represents a logical development of successful experience in a rhythm band, recorder band, or an organization of similar nature.

A varied program that appeals to everyone should be built. If a large group of experienced players is available, they should be helped to organize a band or orchestra. If there are only a few experienced players, they should be encouraged to form a chamber music group. If several people are interested in a dance band, they should be helped to organize one. For persons who have a great deal of leisure time for lessons and practice, piano classes may be offered. For those who have little time for practice and class attendance, a short course in single instruments, such as the ukelele or banjo, may be offered. If a scarcity of players of certain instruments makes impossible a balanced instrumentation for an orchestra, the leader should start a band and organize classes in the scarce instruments.

4. *He obtains necessary facilities and equipment.* The nature of the program determines the kind and quantity of facilities and equipment. They are important only insofar as they contribute to the success of the program. They are means to an end. The recreation leader must not become so involved in securing them that he neglects the program. On the other hand, it is essential that he secure the most adequate equipment possible, and that he make sound plans for extensions and additions as the program expands.

The most essential *facilities* include rehearsal rooms, classrooms, and practice rooms. Activities in the playing program may take place both in rooms devoted solely or largely to music and in rooms used for other purposes. An auditorium or gymnasium, for example, may serve as a rehearsal room for large instrumental organizations, such as bands or orchestras. Rooms of this size are generally unsatisfactory for use by small groups, because of sound distortions.

Rooms used primarily in connection with the playing program range all the way from a band or orchestra rehearsal room to rooms for small instrumental ensembles, rooms for piano classes, rooms for individual practice, and storage rooms. A brief discussion of each of these types of rooms follows. For complete information on music rooms, see *Music Rooms and Equipment* (Revised Edition), Music Education Research Council Bulletin No. 17, which may be obtained from the Music Educators' National Conference (64 East Jackson Boulevard, Chicago).

A room for band or orchestra rehearsal should be large, well lighted, and equipped with risers. There should be at least nine square feet of floor space for each player, his instrument, and music stand. Each player requires 250 cubic feet of air space. The front risers should be 60 inches wide, to accommodate instruments and music stands. The back riser should be 72 inches wide, because of the size of the string basses, kettle drums, and other large instruments, which are usually at the back of the group.

Classes in band and orchestra instruments may use any room of ordinary size, provided the chairs are movable. Piano classes may use any room which has sufficient space for one or more pianos and for the necessary number of silent keyboards. Small instrumental ensembles may use any room large enough to accommodate the players and their instruments.

Any size room may be used for practice, but the use of a large room is a waste of space. The usual sizes of practice rooms are: for band and orchestra instruments, six by eight feet; for piano, with space for one other instrument, eight by ten feet.

It is advisable to have storage space divided into two rooms, one for instruments and one for music. Instruments should be stored in lockers. These may be constructed of wood in various shapes and sizes to accommodate the different instruments. It is possible, also, to purchase steel cabinets which have lockers for storing all sizes and shapes of instruments.

The room for music storage needs shelves for bound books, filing cabinets for sheet music, and racks or tables for sorting music.

Equipment necessary for the playing program includes pianos, silent keyboards, band and orchestra instruments, simple instruments, rhythm instruments, music stands, and chairs. Before buying any musical equipment, the recreation leader should secure the advice of a music specialist, and he should buy only from reputable dealers or responsible individuals.

Grand pianos are always preferable to upright pianos, but are too expensive for general use. For a large room or auditorium, however, a grand piano of appropriate size is almost essential. For practice rooms and rooms of ordinary size, upright pianos are generally adequate. The trend toward having small grands, small uprights, and spinets in homes has resulted in the availability of used large uprights and some large grands at reduced prices. These older pianos are sturdy and suitable for use in the recreation program.

Violins, clarinets, and trumpets are common band and orchestra instruments. Many people who desire to play them already own an instrument or are willing to purchase one. In addition, many persons have such instruments which they no longer use and are willing to lend or give to the recreation program. On the other hand, it is usually necessary to purchase or rent some of the rarer instruments, such as oboes, flutes, bassoons, and tubas.

Rhythm instruments, such as auto-harps, recorders, ukeleles, and ocarinas are generally inexpensive. Most people are eager to purchase the instrument of their choice. The recreation leader, however, should buy a number of these instruments, in order to have them always available for use. Making many of these instruments is a simple matter and may be accomplished by the arts and crafts phase of the recreation program.

Music stands should be of all-metal construction with heavy bases. Most stands need to be adjustable only as to height. The director and the players of a few instruments require stands with an adjustable angle.

5. *He ascertains that the equipment receives proper care and adequate maintenance.* Although the equipment for the playing

program is expensive, it is durable. With proper care and maintenance, it gives years of service. Nevertheless, it is not indestructible and is often subjected to shameful neglect and wanton destruction. One of the major responsibilities of the recreation leader is to supervise the care of equipment to insure that it is used but not abused. In addition, he must make provision for prompt repair of damaged instruments.

Intelligent care and handling represent the biggest factors in prolonging the life of musical instruments. A large number of repair bills result from carelessness and neglect on the part of the player. Suggestions for proper care of instruments follow:

Regular tuning is probably the most important item in the care of pianos. Pianos should be tuned twice a year, more often if they receive hard use. A competent and reliable tuner should be engaged to take care of all pianos on a regular schedule. If he learns to know them and takes an interest in them, he usually does a better job than a tuner who comes in on a single assignment.

Grand pianos should be kept locked, and covered with a regulation piano cover, when not in use. Locking them prevents unauthorized use. Covering them not only keeps out dampness and dirt, both of which are detrimental to the action, but also protects the finish.

A piano in a room used for purposes other than music requires special precautions. For example, a piano in an auditorium or gymnasium is often subjected to the grossest abuse. Many people move it unnecessarily, sit on it, use it as a rack for coats or books, burn it with cigarettes, and play games around it. In order to minimize damage, such a piano should be kept in a corner or some other place where it is well out of the way of other activities. The necessity for safeguarding the piano should be impressed upon all who use the room. If it is a grand piano, it should be mounted on roller frames or trucks to facilitate moving it without damage to its legs or to the floors. An upright piano can be encased in a padded wooden crate, built in sections for easy removal.

Careless handling on the part of the players causes most of

the damage to band and orchestra instruments. The necessity for handling instruments carefully, keeping them clean, and reporting immediately any damage should be urged upon the players. The player of a stringed instrument should wipe his instrument with a clean soft cloth after each use. The player of a wood-wind instrument should swab the bore of his instrument with a dry swab after each use and with an oiled swab once a month. The player of a brass instrument should rinse the tubing of his instrument with warm soapy water once a week, and lubricate the valves and slides frequently. When not in use, smaller instruments should be kept in cases, and larger instruments, for which no case is provided, should be kept in a regulation cover.

Most musical instruments are complex mechanisms which can be irreparably damaged by unskilled repairmen. The services of a responsible firm which specializes in repairing instruments should be secured, and all repair work promptly referred to them. Players should not attempt to make their own repairs, unless they have had special instruction.

6. *He secures the services of competent music specialists to conduct the instrumental organizations and teach instrumental classes.* A successful playing program requires music specialists who are fine musicians and expert teachers. In addition, they must have well-rounded personalities and qualities of leadership that inspire confidence, cooperation, and enjoyment on the part of the group with which they work.

In looking for qualified leaders for the playing program, the entire community and surrounding communities should be explored. The music personnel in schools and colleges offers a rich source of music leadership. These individuals are often willing to extend their activities into the recreation program. Using school personnel has the desirable effect of bringing about coordination and cooperation between the school program and the recreation program. It also encourages the continuation of participation in music on the part of students after they are graduated from school. Church organists and choir directors often are qualified to conduct instrumental groups and to teach instruments. Their experience with adults in choirs and other church activities helps to give them a good outlook on recreational music. Private instrumental teachers and professional musicians are often successful in teaching instrumental classes, but, in engaging their services for the recreation program, the recreation leader should exercise care not to arouse the antagonism of other private teachers or of musicians' unions. Amateur musicians in businesses or professions other than music often gain great satisfaction from working in the playing program. They have the amateur's point of view and provide inspiration and encouragement to other amateurs.

7. *He discovers talented individuals in the playing program and prepares them for leadership.* Every group contains a few persons with special musical talent. If their talent is discovered and properly developed, they can make a vital contribution to the recreation program. Inspired and pleased with their own accomplishment, they approach leading and instructing others with a fresh outlook and contagious enthusiasm.

All the leaders in the playing program should be constantly alert to recognize unusual talent and should take every opportunity to guide and develop it. If a person makes unusual progress in an instrumental class, for example, he should be allowed to assist the regular instructor when a new class begins. He should be encouraged to continue his study of music, and gradually worked into a position of responsibility.

8. *He coordinates the playing program with other community programs and enterprises.* The recreation playing program represents only one phase of the community's cultural program. As such, it should complement existing programs, avoiding duplication of effort. For example, if some other agency already sponsors a community orchestra, it may be inadvisable to start a second orchestra. Under such circumstances, support may be lent to the existing orchestra from whose leader may be ascertained what kind of playing activities would strengthen his organization. If his orchestra lacks violins, for example, a recreation group may be interested

in a violin class and encouraged to join the outside orchestra when it can play sufficiently well.

There should be a free exchange of ideas, personnel, facilities, and equipment with other agencies. The recreation leader should join with them in worth-while cooperative enterprises and work with them in planning and scheduling, to reduce time conflicts to a minimum. Areas of responsibility should be determined so that all community resources are mobilized and utilized for the good of the people.

9. *He integrates the playing program with other phases of his recreation program.* The playing program contributes to the effectiveness of the entire recreation program, and itself gains strength, when integrated with other phases of the program. Playing, singing, and listening go hand in hand. Experience in one of these activities enriches experience in the others. Listening to music is more meaningful if a person has played an instrument. Fine playing has much in common with fine singing; only the medium is different. Experience in all three activities is desirable for every person.

The playing program may furnish varied and unusual accompaniments for community singing and for choral singing. A band or orchestra may be brought into a period of community singing to provide accompaniments and to present a short program. An operetta or musical show may be arranged as a joint effort of singing, playing, and dramatic programs. Choral singing may become a part of the activities of the band or orchestra. Accompanists may prepare in the piano classes to play accompaniments for community singing, choral singing, and voice classes. It may be arranged with the person in charge of arts and crafts to make simple instruments, as a part of his program. Instrumental groups may be brought into the music appreciation classes to demonstrate their instruments and to play short programs.

10. *He arranges for public performances by the instrumental groups.* Public performances give impetus and motivation to the playing program. They also bring about favorable publicity and

public support. Every instrumental group should have the opportunity to perform on occasions directly related to the recreation program and for other community affairs.

The recreation leader should bring the playing program to the attention of the community, by informing civic clubs, schools, churches, and other organizations about the various instrumental groups available for public performances. At least one major program, in which all the instrumental groups participate, should be presented each year. Reciprocal programs with the schools, churches, and other agencies in the community and in surrounding communities should be arranged. The leader should capitalize on the publicity value of National Music Week (usually in May) by planning a series of programs in cooperation with other organizations. He should arrange for public demonstrations of instrumental classes. He should invite a well-known conductor to hold an instrumental clinic, open to all interested instrumentalists in the community. In other words, he should seize every opportunity to enrich the life of the community through instrumental music.

11. *He conducts a training program for leaders in the playing program.* Adequate preparation of recreation leaders is of prime importance. The recreation leader should conduct a continuing program of pre-service and in-service preparation, including institutes, workshops, and conferences. The program to prepare leaders for the playing program should make provision for music specialists who have little or no background in recreation and for recreation specialists whose musical backgrounds are limited.

The music specialists need to become familiar with the general objectives of recreation programs and with the aims and ideals of the particular recreation program in which they are going to work. They need a basic orientation in recreation procedures, the principles of recreation leadership, and their specific duties. They need to be aware of the nature of their relationship to the recreation program and of their responsibility to the people they serve and to other recreation workers. They should have an opportunity to observe expert recreation workers on the job. Finally, they should be able to put what they have learned into practice under the supervision of an experienced recreation worker.

Recreation specialists should have an opportunity to work with experts in recreational music. They need to become aware of the potentialities of music as a recreational activity, and to develop a broad understanding of the unique human values of music. They need to learn how best to use whatever musical skills and talent they may have. Finally, they need to have opportunity to observe an expert recreational music specialist at work and to participate in music themselves.

12. *He maintains an adequate music library for the playing program.* The success of the playing program depends to a great extent on the selection of the finest published material for use in classes and in instrumental organizations. The recreation leader should rely on the judgment of the music specialists in the selection of materials, but he must supervise purchases, to avoid needless duplication. In addition, he must organize an efficient system for storing, checking out, and safeguarding the materials.

SELECTED REFERENCES

RECREATION

FITZGERALD, GERALD B. *Community Organization for Recreation.* New York: A. S. Barnes & Co., 1948.

――――. *Leadership in Recreation.* New York: A. S. Barnes & Co., 1951.

HUTCHINSON, JOHN L. *Principles of Recreation.* New York: A. S. Barnes & Co., 1951.

SLAVSON, S. R. *Recreation and the Total Personality.* New York: Association Press, 1946.

MUSIC (GENERAL)

BAKER, THEODORE. *Biographical Dictionary of Musicians.* New York: G. Schirmer, Inc., 1940.

BARTON, FRED B. *Music as a Hobby.* New York: Harper & Bros., 1941.

BAUMAN, ALVIN. *Elementary Musicianship.* New York: Prentice-Hall, Inc., 1947.

COPLAND, AARON. *Our New Music.* New York: McGraw-Hill Book Co., 1941.

KOLODIN, IRVING. *The New Guide to Recorded Music* (International Edition). Garden City, N.Y.: Doubleday & Co., Inc., 1950.

MCKINNEY, HOWARD D., AND ANDERSON, W. R. *Discovering Music.* New York: The American Book Co., 1934.

NEWMAN, EARNEST. *Stories of the Great Operas.* New York: Garden City Publishing Co., Inc., 1930.

SCHOLES, PERCY A. *The Oxford Companion to Music.* New York: Oxford University Press, 1938.

SIEGMEISTER, ELI. *The Music Lover's Hand Book.* New York: William Morrow & Co., 1943.

SPAETH, SIGMUND. *A Guide to Great Orchestral Music.* New York: Random House, 1943.

LISTENING

BURROWS, RAYMOND, AND REDMOND, BESSIE CARROLL. *Symphony Themes.* New York: Simon and Schuster, 1942.

COPLAND, AARON. *What to Listen for in Music.* New York: McGraw-Hill Book Co., 1939.

HAGGIN, B. H. *Music for the Man Who Enjoys Hamlet.* New York: Alfred A. Knopf, 1944.

HALLSTROM, JOHN. *Relax and Listen.* New York: Rinehart & Co., Inc., 1947.

STRINGHAM, EDWIN J. *Listening to Music Creatively.* New York: Prentice-Hall, Inc., 1946.

TAYLOR, DEEMS. *The Well Tempered Listener.* New York: Simon and Schuster, 1940.

SINGING

CHRISTY, VAN A. *Glee Club and Chorus.* New York: G. Schirmer, Inc., 1940.

DAVISON, ARCHIBALD. *Choral Conducting.* Cambridge, Mass.: Harvard University Press, 1940.

FREISWYK, SIEBOLT H. *Forty Approaches to Informal Singing.* New York: National Recreation Association, 1939.

WILSON, HARRY R. *Lead A Song.* Chicago: Hall & McCreary Co., 1942.

PLAYING

BRAND, ERICK D. *Band Instrument Repairing Manual.* Elkhart, Indiana: H. and A. Selmer, Inc., 1939.

COOKE, CHARLES. *Playing the Piano for Pleasure.* New York: Simon and Schuster, 1941.

JOHNSON, GERALD W. *A Little Night Music.* New York: Harper & Bros., 1937.

MADDY, J. E. *School Bands, How They May Be Developed.* New York: National Bureau for the Advancement of Music, 1931.

————. *School Orchestras, How They May Be Developed.* New York: National Bureau for the Advancement of Music, 1931.

ZANZIG, AUGUSTUS D. *Starting and Maintaining a Community Orchestra.* New York: National Recreation Association, 1940.

————. *Starting and Developing a Rhythm Band.* New York: National Recreation Association, 1937.

INDEX

A

Accordion, 130, 138
Action songs, 69–70, 104, 108–109
Art songs, 27–28, 70, 109–110
Autoharp, 130, 132

B

Bach, Johann Sebastian, 24, 33
Ballet music, 28
Bands, 135–138
    concert, 135
    dance, 136–137
    harmonica, 138
    marching, 135
    recorder, 138
    rhythm, 137–138
Banjo, 130, 131
Bass clarinet, 21
Bass drum, 23
Bassoon, 21
Battery, 22
Beats, conducting, 90–92
Beethoven, Ludwig van, 25, 26
Bizet, George, 31
Brahms, Johannes, 25, 28
Brass instrument ensembles, 139
Brasses, 21–22, 133, 135
Bugle corps, 138
Building a record library, 41–48

C

Cabinet, record, 62–63
Cactus needles, 61
Cadence, 12

Card catalogue for recordings, 63
'Cello, 128
Chamber music, 29
Charpentier, Gustaf, 31
Children's recordings, 55–58
Choral collections, 80–83
    girls' and women's voices, 82
    male voices, 82–83
    mixed voices, 81
Choral programs, director, 74–75
    library, 75
    public performances, 75
    rehearsal rooms, 75
    rehearsals, 75
    requisites for, 74–75
Choral singing, 72–75
Chords, 13, 14
Clarinet, 20, 21, 128, 146
Classes, instrumental, 123–126
    size of, 125
    types of, 128
    orchestra and band instrument, 127–130
    piano, 126–127
    simple instrument, 130
    voice, 75–77
Classicism, 25–26
Col legno, 19
Combined songs, 105, 110
Comic opera, 32
Community orchestra, 134, 135
Community singing, 85
Competitions, 87
Compositions, types of, 26–34
Concert bands, 135
Concerto, 33
Concerts, 34–35
    arranging, 40

Index

R

Recitals, 34–35
 arranging, 40
Recitative, 30
Record cabinets, 62–63
Recorder, 130–131
Recording equipment, selection
   and care, 58–64
Recordings, for adults, 44–54
 art song, 45
 ballet music, 46
 for beginning collections, 42–
   43
 care of, 63–64
 chamber music, 46–47
 for children, 55–58
 choral music, 47
 concerto, 48
 opera, 49–51
 orchestral, 51–52
 overtures, 54
 piano music, 54
 sacred songs, 54
 symphonic poems, 53
 symphonies, 52–53
Recreation, defined, 2
 through listening, 10–37
 and music, 1
 objectives of, 3
 through playing, 122–139
 through singing, 65–84
Recreation leader, and the listening program, 38–41
 and music, 7
 and the playing program, 140–
   154
 and the singing program, 85–
   121
Rhythm, 10–11
Rhythm bands, 137–138
Romanticism, 25–26

Romberg, Sigmund, 32
Rossini, Gioacchino, 30, 32
Rote teaching of songs, 103–104
Rounds, 24, 71, 104–105, 117–
   118

S

Saltando, 19
Sapphire point needles, 62
Schubert, Franz, 26
Schumann, Robert, 27
Selecting recordings, guides for,
   42–44
Simple instrument classes, 130–
   132
Simple instrument ensembles, 139
Singing, choral, 72–75
 community, 65–72
 with a leader, 67–69
 without a leader, 66–67
 part, 106–107
 unaccompanied, 105–106
Singing program, materials for,
   77–84
Sings, guides for planning, 96–
   102
 procedures for, 102–106
Singspiel, 32
Snare drum, 23
Soloist, 101
Sonata, 33, 34
Song books, 101
 for community singing, 78–79
Song leader, repertory for, 107–
   121
Song leading, 102–107
 action songs, 104
 combined songs or vocal com-
   bats, 105
 familiar songs, 102–103
 part singing, 106

· 159 ·